THE BOUNDLESS LIFE

THE
BOUNDLESS
LIFE

13 Lessons Learned the *Hard* Way

SIMON DONATO

Collins

Published by Collins, an imprint of HarperCollins Publishers Ltd

First edition

HarperCollins books may be purchased for educational, business,
or sales promotional use through our Special Markets Department.

HarperCollins Publishers Ltd
2 Bloor Street East, 20th Floor
Toronto, Ontario, Canada
M4W 1A8

www.harpercollins.ca

Library and Archives Canada Cataloguing in Publication
information is available upon request.

ISBN 978-1-44344-655-6

Printed and bound in the United States of America
LSC(C) 9 8 7 6 5 4 3 2 1

To my parents.
My mother gave me the strength,
and my father, the means.

Contents

Introduction

Overcome Your Fear
of Success

everal years ago I had an epiphany while racing . . .

Slow down.

You're going too hard, too fast, too soon.

Remember, he beat you by ten minutes just eight months ago.

Don't attack now; he's only going to run you down later.

Fuck it.

Thirty kilometers later I had beaten one of the best trail runners on the circuit.

What this experience highlighted for me was something that I've struggled with throughout my life—making the decision to commit to something 100 percent. In general, I don't think people are afraid of failure; I think they're afraid of success. Or, more specifically, I think they're afraid of the effort required to attain success. And by "people," I mean you. And me.

When I was a teenager and trying desperately to figure out what the hell to do with my life, I went to my dad for advice. He told me that I could make a living doing anything I wanted. I could be a street performer, an athlete, a scientist, or a lawyer—as long as I was the best at what I did.

"People," he told me, "will *always* pay for the best."

As you might expect, his advice made little sense to my young brain. In fact, I found it more intimidating than comforting. To be honest, I had spent my life to that point staunchly not being "the best" at anything. Confidence was definitely lacking. Sure, I was *good* at lots of things, but greatness eluded me. Ultimately, though, it wasn't that I lacked the talent. I just lacked the will. For example, I was ski racing a lot back then and had the opportunity to travel west to Canada's Rocky Mountains and attend a school that would put me on the slopes every day. Had I truly wanted to be an Olympic-level ski racer, I would have jumped at the opportunity. But at age fourteen, I was too afraid to take the risk. I wasn't the best for my age at my club; I didn't believe in my ability. Of course I *didn't want to fail*, but more important, *I was afraid of putting in the effort required to succeed*. The same was true for football, soccer, baseball, and academics: I was usually good, never great. I was occasionally rewarded with a Most Improved Player acknowledgement but was rarely an MVP.

My recollection of my late teens and twenties was that I followed the path of least resistance in most aspects of my life. I studied kenpo karate for a number of years and was good enough to get my black belt along the way. But despite my desire to emulate my on-screen heroes, I never committed enough to reach their level. Graduate school was much the same. While my peers were writing papers, researching grant applications, and attending conferences, I was planning my next race. Without much distinction, I managed to land a job with a major oil company in Calgary. Life rolled on: I showed up for work each day, put in my eight or nine hours, and, as with most things in my life, operated at a 7.5/10 level. I had many opportunities to be great, but I never seized them—something was always holding me back.

Adventure racing (AR) was the one aspect of my life that I did chase with a fervor that was conspicuously absent from the "important" things that I should have been focusing on. On the invitation of a close friend, I entered my first adventure race at twenty-one years old and immediately fell in love with the sport, where coed teams of four are required to navigate their way through a rugged race course using only human-powered locomotion, maps, and compasses. The courses are usually hundreds of kilometers long, and involve long, minimally supported treks through barren landscapes, mountain biking, paddling, rope work, and more. I had heard reports that these races were brutal sufferfests, with athletes finishing without any skin left on their feet and with blisters that were bigger than toes. They sounded exotic and adventurous, and they seemed like a great way to test myself in a manner that I had never experienced. My passion fueled my drive and I sought—uncharacteristically—to become one of the best adventure racers in the world. For the next eight years, the sport consumed most of my life.

Whereas I struggled to stay totally motivated in academia, I found no trouble turning myself inside out to push my limits on the race course or to lead expeditions. Perhaps it was the restrictions of life—unlike the freedom of sport—that gave me a mental block and interrupted my focus, but somehow on the trails or roads I was able to will myself to overcome the challenges I faced there. Fear didn't seem to impede me. During grad school, I continued adventure racing, transitioning to shorter, sprint-distance races and moving into the top-five teams on the planet with my team, Hammer Nutrition.

When I first began adventure racing, I set a private goal, which was to race at the pinnacle of the sport by the age of twenty-five. That was the year I raced the Eco-Challenge—the de facto Olympics for the sport—finishing a very respectable tenth. I had finally found something that I had a natural talent and a deep passion for. The effort required to be great didn't seem as daunting when the positive results were pouring in. Long hikes, epic rides, and midnight paddles became normal parts of my training regime. The experiences shaped how I viewed myself and the world. The lessons I learned through AR began to seriously influence the decisions I made in the rest of my life. Of course, all of this happened under my nose. I was committed to AR and the lifestyle because I enjoyed it. It wasn't work for me; it was an escape. While other areas of my life felt like work and tended to bore me, adventure, exploration, fitness, and discovery were passions that were only stoked through doing, and the more I did, the more I wanted to do. A funny thing happened during this time: I started to excel in the areas where I had tons of passion.

Yet as I wrapped up my academic career, I began to lose interest in adventure racing, which had steered my life in so many ways since I first started in 1998, and I decided to leave the sport. It was time to move on and I was ready for my next challenge. I also stepped down from the Canadian Adventure Racing Association, which I had founded and run for several years. My interests shifted to running and cycling, as much for their simplicity as for the enjoyment I got from training and competing with my friends. Perhaps it was the training routine. I'm not sure why, but for whatever reason, I began to immerse myself deeply in running and started seeing success there, with podium finishes and steady improvements in my personal-best times.

I moved to Calgary after finishing my PhD to work for Imperial Oil as a petroleum geologist. The job with the oil company would allow me to apply my education and pay me handsomely for doing so—plus I'd get to live in Calgary and near the Rocky Mountains. The decision to move west wasn't without debate, though, as I had an offer from Toronto Fire Services to work as a firefighter at the same time. I had to choose between a job in my field of study that paid very well but had little job security and a job that would come with some physical risks and lower pay but much more job security.

Around the time I was making this career decision, another life-changing moment happened. The famous aviator Steve Fossett went missing while on a pleasure flight in southwestern Nevada. After the failed initial search wound down, I began to wonder if a team of athletes searching high-probability remote areas on foot would have a better chance of finding him. I rolled this idea around in my mind for several months. With the money I was earning from my steady job, I realized that I could organize my own expedition to search for Fossett and his missing plane. This was the project that kickstarted Adventure Science (adventurescience.com), a volunteer organization I started in 2008 that has played a huge role in my life and in setting my current path.

As I moved into my thirties, I was able to put more

money into my passion for adventure and exploration thanks to my career as a geologist. This day job fueled larger adventures and greater projects, including Adventure Science. The search for Steve Fossett may have been our first project, but the seeds for Adventure Science were first planted in 2001 while I was on my first paleontologic field trip as a graduate student. My discovery of what turned out to be the exoskeleton of a new species of eurypterid—an ancient predator of the prehistoric seas analogous to the modern land scorpion, except much larger—made me realize that if we followed the geologic trend away from the road and into the forest, we might be able to discover more specimens. I was intrigued and excited by the idea that stepping off the beaten path could yield incredible discoveries.

The exploration and research I undertook during my PhD fieldwork galvanized my thoughts about how fitness, combined with scientific knowledge and the ability to be a keen observer, could take exploration and discovery to the next level. I thought about the history of exploration and how humans, through a combination of fitness, ingenuity, and technology, had pushed into uncharted realms, exploring, observing, learning. However, somewhere in the last century, we had lost this incredibly important pairing. Overwhelmingly, fitness, in the pursuit of science, had been seemingly replaced by technology. Those who possessed fitness and the desire to push exploration were more commonly embarking on adventures that didn't incorporate any science. I lived in a world where geologists drove from site to site, exploring only what was within steps of their vehicles. I saw field expeditions cost tens of thousands of dollars because of the "need" for helicopters and other expensive add-ons due to the scientists' lack of fitness, endurance, or technical skill. *What if*, I thought, *we used adventure athletes like me to get into and explore these remote and difficult-to-access areas?* I envisioned a program in which the field scientist and subject expert would spend time with athletes, educating them on how to be observers and training them to cover specific routes each day and to record their findings through written notes, photos, videos, and GPS coordinates. The teams would be able to move lightly and quickly through terrain that had stopped researchers in the past and, in doing so, make new discoveries that could then be explored later, at a lower cost, by the experts.

While I finished my dissertation, this idea tumbled around in my brain. I discussed it with other researchers, asking them if they saw any value in having a team of trained athletes assist with their field programs. Although they did see the benefits, they always brought up the same two points: (1) these researchers got into the profession due to their love of fieldwork and would not want to give that up, and (2) the expeditions were already expensive, and they could not afford to bring athletes into the field with them. I realized quickly that if I wanted to do this, and challenge the existing paradigm, I'd have to forge my own path and create this from the ground up. Thankfully, I had very supportive friends who nurtured the idea and helped me develop it. Adventure Science was born. I had found the perfect marriage between adventure racing, exploration, and scientific research.

My introduction to ultrarunning was also a very organic process. Living and working in Calgary as a geologist meant that I was approximately sixty minutes from an endless network of trails in the Canadian Rocky Mountains. With my friends and family, I spent as much free time as I could exploring these trails. Hikes turned to runs and, the next thing I knew, I was ultrarunning. I still didn't consider myself a runner, but I sure loved to run through the mountains and challenge myself. I began to fall in love with running very long distances, and as my passion grew, so did my desire to learn more about the sport of ultrarunning itself, which wasn't yet mainstream at that point.

The idea for *Boundless* didn't simply come to me during a eureka moment. It was the result of an Adventure Science project that I undertook in 2010, when I registered to run in the Canadian Death Race—a 125 km long ultramarathon I'd known about for many years but had previously avoided due to the distance. Go Death Racer was a project that I created to look at the role core strength played in ultrarunning, but I also hired a film crew to document the project. I'd always wanted to create a documentary or television show, and I thought that a film on the race would be a good resource for athletes who were looking to get into the sport and at a loss about where to start, how to prepare, and what to expect in this iconic Canadian race. The project was a huge success. From the athletes and volunteers, we collected a significant amount of data as we tracked how the athletes responded to the distance in terms of discomfort, pain, and injury—comparing the results of the athletes who had done core training and those who hadn't. After logging all the footage, I sent it to my friend Josh Eady, an editor in Toronto, who saw the potential in this documentary for a longer series in which Turbo and I would compete in ultra-endurance races all over the world. Turbo, aka Paul Trebilcock, is a longtime friend and former training partner whom I met while at McMaster University in Hamilton, Ontario. He and his wife had adopted me as their wild and crazy son while I completed my studies. The Canadian network Travel and Escape was interested in our pitch. We couldn't believe our luck. That spring was a blur as we sold the concept and started the planning process and I began my transition out of the oil industry. It was an uncertain proposition, though, as we were contracted to produce ten episodes by December. After that, we didn't know if we'd get another shot.

Walking away from my career as a geologist was definitely a leap of faith, but it was an important one. I hadn't been able to transpose the passion and commitment I had for adventure racing and ultrarunning onto this job or even my marriage, and I had slipped in both. Now it was time to focus on pursuing that which brought me joy. I was charting my own course. I had changed—but didn't realize then how much.

Of all the events and challenges that I've faced and learned from in my life, *Boundless* has been my greatest teacher by far. The scheduling of the season is done to suit a television production schedule—not to favor an athlete. With races of this duration and difficulty, an athlete needs plenty of recovery time. The general rule of thumb is typically three to four weeks of recovery for every hundred miles raced. Not having the luxury of this timeline pushed both Turbo and me physically and emotionally. As I dealt with my recent separation, the challenges of racing and filming, and the management of my knee injury, there were moments when I didn't think I'd be able to finish a race or start the next one. *Boundless* forced me to push hard and to always dig deep. I get a lot of mail from fans of the show and there are two major themes to their responses. The first is that they are inspired to get off the couch and get active. The second is that they really relate to seeing us battle our demons on the race course—as they feel that they get to know us through these struggles. In many ways, our challenges are also their challenges, even if the context for their struggles is different from ours.

Season one of *Boundless* was an experience unlike any other I'd ever faced. Not only did it plunge me into the world of multiday stage racing, but it did so with a schedule that would make any seasoned athlete shake his or her head, because the distances—coupled with the short recovery time—invariably made us less fit over the course of the season. We competed in eight races that first season and traveled over 1,100 human-powered kilometers in the process. Our first race, the Molokai 2 Oahu (M2O), was in late July 2012. It is a famous paddleboard race that covers thirty-two miles between the two islands and crosses the infamous Channel of Bones. Less than a month later, we traveled to Iceland to compete in our first multiday stage running race—the seven-day, 250 km Fire and Ice Ultra. Three short weeks after that, I traveled without Turbo to Kenya to run the Amazing Maasai Marathon, a 75 km run in traditional Maasai territory, near the equator. The following week Turbo rejoined me in South Africa to compete in the Hansa Fish River Canoe Marathon, a two-day, 80 km whitewater kayak race near the town of Cradock. A week later we were in Hurricane, Utah, to compete in a mountain bike race called 6 Hours of Frog Hollow. After a welcomed three-week break, we were on the road again, this time to Egypt to compete in what is still one of my top-three toughest races, the seven-day stage running race called the Sahara Race, which winds 250 kilometers through the Sahara Desert. Three weeks after the Sahara Race we were off to Asia for our final two events—the Ancient Khmer Path ultramarathon stage race in Cambodia, followed a week later by the Laguna Phuket Ironman 70.3 event in Thailand. By December 3, 2012, we had successfully, and somewhat miraculously, wrapped the first season. I was physically spent and Turbo was emotionally exhausted, but we had survived and maintained our strong friendship through-out. Though exhilarating, those four months were the hardest of my life.

Since that last race, we've shot another two seasons and are up to twenty-seven full races and over four thousand kilometers of human-powered racing. We've continued to have ups and downs, dealing with the challenges that come with filming, racing, injuries, bad weather, and more. To spice things up, we added two hosts in our third season, which contributed another layer of issues, as we had to mesh personalities and sort out more logistics when film-ing. I've learned a lot about myself during these three sea-sons, as every challenge we face during *Boundless* can be related to our regular lives at some level and provides life lessons. It's certainly made me more introspective, as I have much more control of the direction my life will take. I've met a lot of wise people on my journey and have tried to listen and learn. I've realized that we can't overemphasize the importance of doing things that make us happy. While racing can be a distraction from our daily lives, it also helps remind us what we are physically and mentally capable of. It gives us goals and structure, and it pushes us to see where our limits lie. *Boundless* showed me that most of our limits are mental and, with the right attitude, we can push ourselves further than we ever thought possible. No matter the situation, a tired body will almost always follow a determined mind.

Racing has been an excellent teacher for me and, unsurprisingly, it was my most difficult races that taught me the most important lessons. When I train hard or race, I'm able to find a quiet serenity, one that eludes me in the other parts of my life. This mental calmness gives me clarity to focus, think, listen, and learn. Life lessons like perseverance, accepting coaching, staying positive, and being adaptable have come out of these experiences—sometimes in very visceral ways.

Even so, sometimes we still need a catalyst in life to make the huge mental leaps and realizations. I had mine in September 2014, when I was invited to speak to a group of runners on the eve of the Wine Country Half Marathon in beautiful Kelowna, British Columbia. I wanted to give the audience something motivational and inspirational. Racking my brain for something relevant, I realized that I had all the motivational material I needed, thanks to a race I had run a few weeks before. What's more, in that single, gorgeous, eureka moment, I realized that I had overcome my lifelong fear of success. And it came at no better place for me: on the trail.

I was competing in a running race called the Iroquois Trail Test (ITT), a rugged 34 km race along the Niagara Escarpment near Toronto that had been on my bucket list for years. The ITT is special because it takes racers through some gnarly, ankle-biting terrain as it snakes along an uplifted limestone plateau running 900 kilometers from Niagara Falls to Tobermory. Going into the race, I knew I'd be lining up against some very fast athletes, including one in particular who had beaten me in a trail race the previous fall. I was anxious for a rematch.

The race began as most do: fast. Four of us shot out to the front immediately and quickly gapped the rest of the field. Within two kilometers, the eventual race winner had sprinted well out of sight on the single track. I found myself running behind my nemesis—matching his quick pace but still feeling strong and able. The pace frightened me, though, and I began to question myself. Was I going too hard, too early? Would this be disastrous later in the race? Surely I *shouldn't* be running with this guy, who eight months earlier had won my hometown trail race and beat me by more than ten minutes on a shorter, easier course. As it had done my entire life, self-doubt was flooding my mind.

And yet, the kilometers ticked by and I stayed on his tail. As we approached the first section of rock hopping, he slowed substantially. For no conscious reason, I did the same. I knew I could easily run this section much more quickly without expending more effort, but I was tormented with doubt. It was far too early to try to pass a guy who was a better runner than me. *Don't attack now; he's only going to run you down later.* Besides, the pace was comfortable and easy. Yet at the same time, another part of me started talking. *Go for it; pass this guy and run for your life.* This time, I decided to listen.

After running a few more uncomfortably slow steps I passed my nemesis and began running as though my life depended on it. It hurt. I redlined. I pushed the downhills. I pushed the climbs. I pushed the flats. For the next thirty kilometers, I ran like an Olympic medal was on the line. I suffered. My legs and lungs burned, but I kept the needle buried.

Not only was I able to hold him off, but I put over five minutes into him by the time I crossed the finish line in second place. I was happy but also somewhat shocked. I had beaten one of the best trail runners in Canada.

Well, the significance of my achievement didn't hit until several weeks later, on the eve of my talk in Kelowna. It struck me like a lightning bolt: I was more afraid of putting in the effort to succeed than I was of failing. Suddenly my dad's words of wisdom—spoken to me over twenty-five years before—made sense. We *can* be anything we want in life and *can* make a living at it if we give our best.

I now believe that we're not afraid of failing as much as we are afraid of committing our minds and bodies to a singular vision, for as long as it takes, no matter how difficult the road may be. This, for me, is the difference between fearing failure and fearing success. Fearing failure keeps us from trying something because we can't handle failure as an outcome. Fearing success prevents us from attempting something because we don't want to put the effort forward that's required to achieve success. So what does success look like? For me, it looks like long days and long nights, exhaustion, setbacks, hurdles, naysayers, and yes, even self-doubt. It looks like years of effort, unwavering belief, and undaunted commitment. For, ultimately, if you want something bad enough, you *will* succeed. Failure? Those are just the lessons I learn along the way that will ultimately help me to become successful.

Someone once said, "When you want to succeed as bad as you want to breathe, then you'll be successful." My forty years on this planet and my observations of my own experiences, as well as those of people close to me, suggest that this is the only way to achieve success and reach your goals.

1.

The Worst Races Are Often the Best Teachers

In races, and in life, we ride a wave of highs and lows, as the intense schedule of *Boundless* reminded me again and again. What goes up, must come down, and vice versa. Knowing this always brought me comfort during my darkest moments on the race course and always helped temper my best moments, which I think kept me grounded (although the Eady brothers and Turbo may have a different opinion!). I also found that my best races were not necessarily my greatest teacher—my worst races were. When you have a good race, you tend not to reflect on it as much as you do when you have a poor race. A win means that everything went as planned and worked well, and there is little to improve on, whereas a major implosion results in some intense soul-searching and going back to the drawing board.

When we shot the first *Boundless* episode, we really had no clue what we were getting into. My ego outshone my ability in some ways. Our first race was the famous

Molokai 2 Oahu Stand Up Paddleboard race across fifty-three kilometers of open Hawaiian ocean, island to island. I had been looking for an epic paddling race to put in the calendar and stumbled on this one—essentially the world championship of endurance paddling—in a sport that neither Turbo nor I had tried. This has become one of our most infamous episodes. We've received the most positive and negative feedback on this one due to our performance—or lack thereof, I should say. Less than one month before the race, neither Turbo nor I had ever stood on a stand up paddleboard (SUP), let alone paddled one. We lived in blissful ignorance of the beating to come. Because I was 90 percent certain I'd be quitting my job as a geologist to go full-time with the show, I'd been trying to wrap up the projects I was working on at the time and, as a result, the SUP training I had planned took a backseat, with running and gym sessions serving as my main workouts. I recall being out on a 50 km training run in the mountains around Canmore with good friends Phil Villeneuve and Matthew Innis and telling them about the race. The consensus was that, without spending any time on the board in advance, I was going to get annihilated, as Turbo and I had initially planned to solo the race. Naïve and undeservedly overconfident, I bet Phil a case of wine that I wouldn't DNF (Did Not Finish) or come DFL (Dead Fucking Last).

I went to Toronto for a quick visit before heading off to Hawaii, during which time I had a few hours of coaching from my friend and national-level paddle instructor Bill Trayling. Although I still didn't know it at the time, paddling on a lake is very different from paddling on the ocean. I left Canada confident that my endurance was going to carry me through this new sporting challenge. Mentally, I saw myself as a dark-horse contender, convinced that no other paddler out there could run fifty kilometers in one shot and therefore wouldn't have the stamina to paddle that distance as fast as I could. Failing was the furthest thing from my mind.

We spent the first few days of our trip exploring Honolulu and Waikiki before heading to Maui, where we were quickly connected with then-seventeen-year-old SUP pro Slater Trout; his friend and sponsor, SUP surf expert Dave Boehne; and Talia Decoite (née Gangini), an eighteen-year-old budding SUP star. We met them at the beginning of the holy grail of downwind paddling, the Maliko run—a ten-mile downwind paddle known for its consistent northeast winds.

The first few hundred meters out of the starting bay were fine. I was surprised to see the guys get on their knees when they entered the open water but followed suit and negotiated some rocks near the mouth of the bay. The water was moving in rolling waves. Some were breaking, but they didn't look that crazy to me. Once I got into the open water, though, it was a different story. Neither Turbo nor I could stand on the board for longer than a few seconds. The nonstop undulations of the conveyor belt that was the ocean that day destroyed my balance, and I was constantly in the water. The paddling I did manage was mostly on my knees or seated. Standing was literally not an option. I was in shock, and my confidence shattered. Here we were about to film our first episode and I couldn't see how either one of us would ever be able to finish. We were terrible. It was physically painful falling and landing on the board numerous times, and I rubbed my chest and ribs raw on the deck as I repeatedly pulled myself back up like an awkward walrus. Helpless, I felt a fear of failure start to grow inside of me as I realized this race was much more than an endurance contest. A successful SUP racer here was equal parts endurance paddler and surfer—both very foreign to me.

We didn't finish the first run, bailing out several miles early. I was worried about the episode—as was the production team. Steven, our producer, made the call to put us on a team instead of having us continue our plan of going solo, which was a good move. Suddenly the prospect of paddling a SUP fifty-three kilometers across the open ocean, in an area that would be five times bigger than Maliko, was looking impossible. That night I had to put my fears to rest and dig deep to dredge up some courage to talk myself into getting on the board again. I was battling a lot of negative emotions and self-doubt. I felt foolish for speaking so arrogantly about a sport I knew nothing about. It was humiliating in a lot of ways, but I knew that quitting was not an option. I was embarking on what amounted to the opportunity of a lifetime and couldn't simply turn my back on it for fear of failing or, worse, humiliating myself on television. I decided I would take what little time I had left before the race and use it to train and practice as much as I could. I wouldn't go down without a fight.

I was up early the next morning and back on the water, paddling the protected harbor of Kahului. I spent an hour on the board and started to rebuild my shattered confidence and improve my balance and skill. I didn't have much time, as we were slated to cycle the massive climb to Haleakalā Crater, a ten-thousand-foot volcano, in the afternoon to catch some sunset shots. It turned out to be one of the most beautiful sunsets I've ever experienced.

The following day we were back on the water with a new 12' 6" SIC (Sandwich Islands Composite) board that had a better profile for wave riding than the 14' Rogue we'd been using. Our previous board had a flat water profile and was constantly submerging under the waves, making it harder to balance. My confidence was growing, and our abbreviated paddle on the Maliko run was a much better experience than our first attempt, with both Turbo and me standing longer and swimming far less. We were moving in the right direction and, depending on your definition of success, it was starting to look like we might achieve some version of it. At this point, success was simply making small improvements. Facing my fear of success here would mean putting in the physical effort and accepting the countless falls, bumps, and bruises that would come with learning.

Our time on Maui drew to a close, but before we left, we met a paddle coach for a blessing—which was a really deep and emotional experience for me, as he asked the ocean to grant us safe passage and for our ancestors to watch over us and keep us safe. My thoughts drifted to my grandparents, long since gone, and I wondered if they would have actually taken pride in my athletic accomplishments. The moment passed, and we headed to catch the ferry to Molokai to prepare for the race. Riding the ferry over was our first experience in the open channel and it was an eye-opener as swells pitched the large boat around like a toy and wave spray easily crested the observation deck we were on. We both realized that we were going to face a lengthy and grueling test the following day.

I was quiet, reflective, and focused that night as I prepped my nutrition and hydration for the following day.

I opted for a mix of real food, such as sandwiches, with bars, gels, and other carbohydrate-rich fuels, which would replace the sugars I was burning on the water. For hydration, it was a mix of electrolyte drinks and some "treats" like Red Bull and Coke. Picking the right food is key to success. Not only does the nutritional value play a major role, but there is an art to picking the food you know you'll want and can stomach at ten, twenty, or fifty kilometers into a challenge—variety is essential for this reason. It's amazing the motivational power that food and drink can have on a tired athlete. Turbo and I had decided to alternate paddling in fifteen-minute intervals in order to stay fresh and strong, with Turbo starting the race, since he was having the most success on the water during training. Despite being older and less muscular, he had better balance on the board.

Race morning was a unique experience. After a light breakfast and a few Gravol pills—which Turbo declined, saying, "I don't get seasick, dude"—we headed down to the beach. An armada of boats floated offshore in the quiet bay, while Jet Skis zipped between them and back and forth to shore, ferrying people and equipment. Our fishing boat was captained by a charter fisherman named Brendt Chang, who had supported racers for years and knew the water inside and out. He was the perfect man to guide our novice team. We had a Jet Ski with us to help us with the transitions between fifteen-minute paddling stints. Hundreds of people buzzed about the beach, loading or unloading last-minute items from their support boats or simply standing in awe at the spectacle before them. A megaphone crackled and the race organizers asked the athletes to form a large circle, hold hands, bow heads, and share in a prayer for the spirits of our ancestors to give us strength to continue paddling when we were depleted. At the time, I had no idea how much additional strength I would need that day.

We had a relaxed start and eased into it, with Turbo and I having reasonable success standing as we paddled the first few miles out of the bay. Our transitions were going well and we were happy and confident. The water was warm, so our falls weren't chilling us. Every fifteen minutes Turbo would swap on or off the board. The swells were bigger here than at Maliko, but the waves weren't breaking—they were like two-story bumps that moved underneath us. We would try to stand as a swell came under the board and then paddle hard to be able to ride down the back side of it, which the pros would surf, conserving energy and dancing easily on the board to maximize their glide.

After racing for ninety minutes, we were paddling off course, unable to fight to cross the prevailing swell direction, and, according to Brendt, heading toward Tahiti instead of

Oahu. Brendt dragged us back on course and we continued. I had been paddling for my fifteen minutes and was expecting a change with Turbo that was slow in coming. At this point, I was spending most of the time paddling on my knees and, with this technique and the course correction, we were technically disqualified—not that anyone was around to observe, as the flotilla was miles in front of us. There was no way we were going to quit, though. I continued to paddle, fully expecting the Jet Ski to zip Turbo over at any moment. Because of the size of the swells, which had grown big enough (fifteen to twenty feet high) to hide the boat when we were both sitting in the trough of a wave, the boat had to keep its distance, so I had no idea why Turbo wasn't coming out.

Nearly an hour had passed before I got close enough to the boat to ask why Turbo wasn't switching with me. Our director, Josh, replied, "He's seasick. He's out." "What do you mean he's out?" I shouted back. Apparently, the pitching seas had got the best of him and he was out of commission, incredibly nauseated, and barely able to sit up. He was lying on the bench in the middle of the boat and not moving. If only he had taken the Gravol pills. I grabbed some food and a hat and pushed off, angry and now more determined than ever not to fail at this challenge. I wasn't going to let the Channel of Bones get the best of us.

I was paddling exclusively on my knees now, which had rubbed raw on the deck of the board. My joints were stiff, my hands blistering, and the sun was burning my skin. With the fifteen-minute alternating schedule that we'd held earlier, I had been able to reapply sunscreen during the breaks and take care of myself better. Now, unexpectedly shouldering the entire load, I was alone—with only the occasional encouragement of our Jet Ski driver to motivate me. None of it mattered, though. I was in the zone and just kept paddling. When my chest and arms started cramping, I changed my stroke to try to use different muscles. One physical barrier after another presented itself. I figured out ways around them, all while maintaining a slow but steady pace forward. Soon I was in the middle of the channel and could no longer see either Molokai or Oahu. The water was a deep azure color and appeared bottomless. I had a sense of how helpless someone lost at sea must feel.

Minutes became hours and, eventually, Oahu came into sight as I bobbed along. Turbo was starting to feel better at this point. I had been paddling on my own for over four hours and was happy to give him a turn and go grab some fuel. Turbo and I swapped several more times as we neared Oahu, its massive volcanic cliffs rising sharply in front of us, its black shoreline subject to the relentless beating of the waves.

It was during one of these swaps that the ocean imparted its final lesson, leaving me with a permanent reminder of its power and the need to take it seriously. Turbo had just relieved me and I was being ferried back to the boat by the Jet Ski for a break and to refuel. The waves were still large. As we approached the swim platform, which hung from the back of the fishing boat, we suddenly found ourselves underneath it. As the boat was lifted high on the crest of a large wave, we sunk into the trough. The boat crashed down onto the back of the Jet Ski and my extended left leg, pinning it just above the ankle for a moment until the next wave carried the boat off of us and our now partly submerged Jet Ski. I yanked my ankle free and grabbed it instinctively, not wanting to look at what I thought could be a very bad injury or fracture. A sharp pain emanated from where it had been pinned. Was it broken? Cut? How badly was I injured? Would I be able to paddle? Was my *Boundless* journey already over? A million thoughts raced through my mind—most of them worry and doubt.

I was talking during this time, although I don't recall making any sounds, and the crew helped me aboard. The first glance at my ankle didn't show much, aside from a two-inch-long gash, which hadn't yet started to bleed. As I examined my foot, I was incredibly relieved to find that there was no sign of any damage worse than that deep cut, which I treated and bandaged over the next thirty minutes before I returned to the water. Although I like to avoid getting injured while racing or training, accidents like this do have the benefit of snapping me back to reality and making me realize how fickle Lady Luck can be. Yes, I consider escaping with only a gash very lucky and am grateful! I suppose it's a perspective thing. You can only shoot yourself through the eye of a needle so many times before you eventually clip the side. Through the drama, though, we continued our slow march toward Oahu.

We were in the homestretch, with a few miles left to paddle. We had been told that this section of the race was the hardest due to the winds blowing in your face instead of at your back, but for me, it was heaven (plus the wind wasn't really that bad at all). The water inside the bay was much calmer, pleasure boaters cheered as they drove by, and people surfed and played in the waves in the distance. I was finally able to stand on my sore and tired legs, stiff from over six hours of kneeling. Turbo let me have the glory of the finish in recognition of me doing the lion's share of the paddling while he was sick, so, with my head held high, I paddled toward two inflatable cubes in the distance, which marked the finish line.

I was already mentally celebrating as I moved inside of the final kilometer of the race when our Jet Ski came racing out toward me, pulling up alongside the board.

Bones Heal and Chicks Dig Scars

I've always been a daredevil but have definitely paid the price with a long list of injuries, many of them caught on home video. In my youth, they were mostly sports injuries, but since then I've managed to add some wear-and-tear injuries that come with age, mileage, and the odd crash. My list includes

eight concussions,
one broken nose,
four broken ribs,
one broken finger,
two broken thumbs,
at least three herniated vertebrae,
one badly torn knee ligament,
one separated shoulder,
countless scars,
multiple severe contusions, and, recently,
one fractured sesamoid bone.

Although I wouldn't wish this litany of injuries on anyone, it has given me a perspective that has served me very well as an athlete: bones (and soft tissue, ligaments, and tendons) heal and chicks dig scars. Seriously, though, every injury I've ever had, no matter how severe, has healed, and after proper rehabilitation, I was able to continue racing and adventuring at a competitive level, often coming back stronger than before the injury.

"Get on the back," our driver said.

"What?"

"Hold your paddle, hop on the back of this, and I'll grab your board."

"Why?" I answered, still confused about his request.

"They are taking the finish line down and they're worried that they won't get a shot of you crossing the line if we don't bring you in quickly."

I was felt like I was being robbed. After battling my own demons and the ocean for nearly nine hours, they were going to tow me to the finish for the shot? *Fuck them*, I thought. I want to do this on my own. But then I shelved my bruised ego and reminded myself that we weren't here to watch me race; we were here to film a TV show. I grudgingly accepted the tow. (We agreed as a team following the M2O that, no matter what, the production team would never interfere in a race again as they had with the final Jet Ski—and three seasons later, we've been able to keep that vow.) The Jet Ski pulled me to within a few hundred meters of the finish and I jumped back in the water to paddle the rest of the way. The race organizers were in the process of dismantling the finish line and, by then, had already brought in one of the finishing buoys and were taking the finishing banner down. I was one of the last paddlers on the water and there was no glory in that.

I paddled my final few strokes, letting the board glide onto shore before stepping off, and touched land again for the first time in nearly nine hours. Hugs, laughter, and some disbelief followed in short order. Despite the fact that we had been disqualified many hours earlier, and that I had taken a tow in the final kilometer, finishing that race was an incredibly sweet feeling. I had never competed in an event in which I had no idea what I was doing. This was completely outside the box for me. To put it in perspective, it would be like racing in the Mountain Biking World Championships having never ridden a bike before. This was a race where I had to go back to the well of courage many, many times. I knew that I was mentally tough, but when you realize that you are completely out of your league and that, no matter what, you'll be in for a grueling day, it's hard to stay positive and confident, which are essential mind-sets in sport. I was proud of myself for pushing on when, after the first day on Maliko, I had wanted to quit. This was a savage way to start *Boundless. It can only get easier from here*, I thought to myself. Turbo went home and told his family that it was the most brutal thing he had ever done. I went home to Canmore and paid off my wine debt. If we only knew what was in store for us . . .

Nine weeks later I found myself in Laikipia, Kenya, and without Turbo. He had a charity event to plan and execute during the same time frame as this race. I was entered in the Amazing Maasai Marathon, a 75 km charity running race in rural Kenya to support the education of local girls. This was my first visit to this part of Africa and I was excited to experience the Maasai culture, having studied it when doing my undergraduate degree in anthropology. I was entering this race with some trepidation, as my knee was sore coming out of the 250 km, weeklong stage running race in Iceland almost a month earlier. I had started experiencing a stabbing pain under my kneecap in the final stage of that race, and I later discovered it was patellar tendinitis or "jumper's knee," a common running ailment for high-mileage athletes. The knee was acutely painful for the three weeks following the race, but it had started to improve shortly before I left for Kenya. My fingers were crossed.

Our first few days in the Maasai heartland were incredible. Interacting with the Maasai and experiencing their traditional life, I joined ceremonial activities, slept on a bed of sticks in a Maasai family's cow-dung hut, and traveled with them on a safari adventure—all major highlights of the trip. As usual, race day saw us rise before the sun to eat and prepare. Sometimes you can just tell it's going to be one of those days straight out of the gate. After a short and terrible sleep, I arrived late to the breakfast tent to find that the other hungry racers had snapped up all of the food. I ended up eating something that resembled beans mixed with cornmeal. It wasn't delicious, and it certainly didn't satisfy my appetite.

I had a short bus ride to the race start in a nearby village while my crew followed behind on ATVs. Josh and Jordan, who were riding together, somehow got lost attempting a shortcut through the myriad elephant trails and cattle paths that bisected the savannah, and they nearly missed the start. The race was like no other I'd ever participated in, as the field was mostly school-aged children, many under the age of ten. It was so inspiring to see these children running happy and free along the dirt roads and trails that formed the course. In addition to the ultra, there was a half marathon and a full marathon option. Most children were entered in the half marathon and ran in their red race shirts. Pinned to many shirts were paper signs championing messages about equality and gender. I was running alright, but these kids were strong and fast. Many of them easily outpaced me in the early kilometers of the race. I was seriously impressed and humbled.

Despite the sun's low position in the sky at the start of the race, the air temperature was hot, and as the morning wore on, it got hotter. I finished the half marathon feeling good. The knee was holding up, I was running steadily, and I was happy. I didn't have a ton of pep, but this was a great race so far. However, as I pushed on toward the marathon distance, I began to struggle to keep my pace up. I'm not sure whether it was the heat, the hilly terrain, or three weeks of no running, but I was slowing down. I limped into the marathon finish with my face looking like a cherry tomato, then refueled in preparation for the final 33 km push. Three kilometers later, I felt a slight twinge in my knee, and the pain that I had been dreading began to reappear. At first it felt like a distant pulse—almost an itch—which then had me wondering if it was a new problem. As five more kilometers passed by (twenty-five remaining), my knee pain worsened until I was in constant pain. The same patellar tendinitis that had appeared during the Fire and Ice Ultra had returned. Although I was no longer enjoying the heat (my Suunto watch showed 40°C or 104°F) or the experience, I pushed on. I had to. If I dropped, there would be no episode, and I also didn't want to be a quitter. Although I had won my last race, I was really starting to slow down, and my ego was again on the ropes and taking a beating. I wondered what success would look like in this race, and if I would even be able to make another twenty-five long, hot, and painful kilometers to the finish.

I continued on like this, running as much as I could but walking more and more, especially on the downhill stretches, which were particularly painful. I was feeling dejected and sorry for myself as I walked down a dusty, red dirt road and came upon a herd of cows that were standing in the middle of it, blocking my path. I had no patience for any delays at this point and, emotionally numb from enduring my knee pain, just walked into the middle of the herd, scattering them as I moved forward. On the other side, unbeknownst to me, were Josh and Jordan. They had been stuck there for over ten minutes, they said, too afraid to move forward for fear of angering the cattle and having them charge their ATV.

We started chatting as I walked, Josh drove beside me, and Jordan filmed. After sharing their adventures thus far, as well as some race updates and gossip, Josh asked me if I wanted to drop, fearing that pushing for the final twenty kilometers would ruin my knee and potentially the rest of the season. After all, we still had a two-day kayak race and a six-hour mountain bike race on the next two weekends, and then two more huge stage running races, and a half Ironman soon after. There would be no time for my injury to recover. Until that point, I really hadn't thought seriously about it. I told him to give me a few minutes to mull it over.

I walked on my own for a while, thinking about how I would likely make my knee worse by continuing to race on it and considering the reasons for and against quitting.

After some time, I concluded that pushing on would invariably result in a bigger injury, longer recovery time, and a greater risk that I wouldn't be able to complete upcoming races. Logically, it didn't make any sense to continue. I decided to cut my losses, and when I caught up to Josh, I told him I was done. The moment after you make the tough decision to abandon a race, all you want to do is get off the course and shower/eat/sleep. I wanted to hop on the quad and get a ride out of there.

Josh said, "I'd never push you to continue if it's going to make you worse, Simon, but why don't you just walk to the next aid station, which is about a kilometer up the hill, and you can drop there? It will be a better end for the episode." I agreed and kept walking.

The aid station was located atop a large hill on the edge of a small village, which amounted to little more than a cluster of dung and grass huts. It was situated around fifty-five kilometers into the race, with twenty kilometers left to go. Several of the villagers were there, volunteering. I walked up to the station and grabbed a drink and some food. I was the first non-Kenyan runner through. I stood there, trying to work up the nerve to withdraw from the race. Every running step I took, it felt like someone was driving a nail into my knee, but surprisingly, I could walk without much pain. I must have looked like hell because one of the women volunteering asked me if I wanted a massage. Still thinking that I'd be pulling the plug momentarily, I agreed and sat down. *Ah, what the hell, I thought, I could use a pick-me-up after this beating.* She got to work on me, massaging out my quads and calves. It felt incredible. As I sat there, I began to reconsider my decision to withdraw. I started thinking about the past year. I remembered how lucky I was to be living this life, which I had dreamed of since my first Eco-Challenge in 2001 and had worked so hard to create. I thought about how I had quit on my marriage with Ally months earlier and how I had quit my job as a geologist, mentally checking out long before I actually left the company. Finally, I looked at this woman, who was smiling, cheerful, and full of encouragement. She had given her time and energy to support the race and its athletes. She was hopeful for us. I felt a lump grow in my throat. I fought it back. Here I was, a wealthy North American running amongst a group of impoverished but happy athletes and villagers in the middle of nowhere, and because the race wasn't going my way, I was going to throw in the towel. I suddenly couldn't do it. I couldn't quit. Finishing this race now felt like a spiritual mission that I had to complete at any cost. In that instant, I redefined what success looked like in this race and made the decision to continue.

I pushed myself to my feet, thanked her for the massage, and resumed my walk. My knee continued to hurt like hell when I ran, so I power-walked as fast as I could. I was sick of this race and just wanted to get it done. Every step brought me closer to the finish line. I used to think that, with several victories to my credit, fifty-mile races were my best distance, but only three races into this *Boundless* odyssey I was turning in my worst performance at that distance. I tried to push these disappointing thoughts out of my head. I started to run—an action that resembled more of a skip-hop as I entered the final five kilometers. I was determined now to push as hard as my body would allow, right to the finish line. When the pain was too much to continue running, I would power-hike for a few minutes, and then try to run again. The pain was my companion, and strangely, I found solace in it—and purpose—as I battled to quell the negative thoughts and overcome my new limitations. It wasn't pretty, but another lump welled up in my throat as I made my way down the final stretch through town, taking the last turn down the finishing straight. As I ran toward the finish line, Paul, one of my Maasai friends, joined me and ran me in, for a time of 9:21. The winner, a Kenyan named Victor Wachira Miano, finished in 4:57. Due to a lack of funding, he's a runner we will likely never see race the Western States Endurance Run or the Ultra Trail du Mont-Blanc (UTMB), despite his incredible speed and talent. Somehow, I managed to hold off the other westerners and was the first foreign finisher. Since that race, I've found it interesting how we celebrate our primarily white North American and European ultra stars to the exclusion of a deep pool of incredibly fast African runners like Victor, who without funding or sponsorship will never be able to afford to travel to the biggest and highest-profile races in order to take on the stars of the sport. Ultras rarely pay, and for Kenyan athletes racing for their survival, if there's no money, then there is no point in racing.

Despite the fact that I didn't have a great day of racing time-wise, this was probably one of the best races I've ever had for my soul. With the odds stacked against me, I thought I was done. I was ready to throw in the towel, but a small act of kindness and some soul-searching brought me back from the brink and carried me to the finish. I ran those final painful kilometers on raw emotion and guts—sometimes that's all you have and all you need. Even in the face of logic and reason, sometimes you need to listen to your gut, follow your heart, and go for it. I redefined my notion of success on that day; in crossing the finish line I couldn't have been more proud of the accomplishment, and the cold Tusker lager handed to me at the finish line was probably one of the best beers I ever drank. I was in heaven. I realized that there was no shame in not being competitive that day. In fact, I was prouder and learned more about myself than I would have if I had run a perfect race with few problems.

2.

Half the Battle
Is Taking the First Step

Have you heard the saying *Luck is what happens when opportunity meets preparation?* News flash: achieving your goals takes time. Sometimes things happen quickly, but more often than not, you need to be patient and observant in order to recognize and take advantage of your golden opportunity when it comes along.

During the summer of 1998, I got a phone call from a good friend of mine, Pete Cameron. Pete had landed a summer job working for Frontier Adventure Racing (FAR), a company helmed by David Zietsma, who was (along with his teammates) arguably Canada's best expedition racer at the time.

I had first heard about the sport of adventure racing the previous year while reading a *Men's Health* magazine article about the planet's ten toughest races. One of the races was called the Eco-Challenge, an event created by then-unknown promoter Mark Burnett (who later went on to create *Survivor*). It was an expedition-style race based on the Raid Gauloises, a French event Burnett had competed in years earlier. I was hooked on the idea of this grueling, exotic sport but had no idea where to begin. At the time, I was just a twenty-one-year-old undergrad student at Western University in London, Ontario.

During that phone conversation with Pete, I found out that FAR was planning a thirty-six-hour event near Fort-Coulonge, Quebec, called Raid the North. Pete told me that I needed to enter this race, FAR's inaugural event. All I could see were the reasons why I shouldn't, and at the time, I could not visualize successfully making this happen. I countered that there was no way I'd be able to put a team together for it. I also didn't have all the required skills. Navigation, in particular, was out of my comfort zone. I knew how to bushwhack, mountain bike, and paddle, and I figured I could learn how to rappel, but detailed map and compass work were new to me, despite my years as a Boy Scout.

He helped me team up with our high school buddy Derek Caveney. In addition to being a varsity cross-country star in university, Derek had been the smartest kid in our graduating class, so Pete figured that we could delegate the navigating to him. That left us with half a team to build. Even if I could find another guy to join our team, where would I find a fit female who would consider a thirty-six-hour rumble through the forests of the Pontiac Ouest region of the Ottawa Valley a good way to spend a weekend? Thankfully, Pete had an answer for that, too. He found a couple of students in the Ottawa area, Heather Breen and Tom Hyde, who were keen to race and looking for team-mates. He could make it all happen, he told me. All I needed to do was to come up with my share of the $1,000 entry fee and get myself and my gear to Quebec. Pete, as it turns out, has been one of my greatest enablers. When I reflect on this entire process, I realize that saying yes to this opportunity was a pivotal moment in my life. That race, in many ways, has shaped the man I've become and the life path I've taken. Although I was nervous, green, and unsure, I recognized the golden opportunity in front of me and took a chance. The worst-case scenario in my mind was either not finishing or somehow losing out on the few hundred dollars that the race cost me. The key for me was recognizing this as an opportunity to step through an open door and into a world that intrigued me. Sure, it wasn't the Eco-Challenge, but it was a step toward it.

The race had a thirty-six-hour time limit for finishing the 150 km nonstop course and it involved five disciplines: a 32 km trek, followed by 25 km of canoeing, a 78 km mountain bike, a Tyrolean (zipline) traverse, and 15 km of whitewater rafting. The rules of the race were pretty straightforward—all teams were required to remain within a hundred meters of each other at all times. If one or more members dropped from the race, the team was automatically unranked but could choose to continue. As in all races, all teams were required to carry mandatory personal gear and mandatory team gear—more on the challenges of assembling and carrying gear in the next chapter. Each team was allowed to have a support member or two, who would transport the gear between each transition area (TA), prepare food, and ensure that the team stayed well fueled and hydrated when passing through the TAs. The 150 km route was denoted by a series of checkpoints (CPs), some of which were also TAs, where we would switch from one discipline to the next. In order to allow for the tracking of teams on course and for the race organizers to have an idea of team ranking, each team received a paper passport that they were required to carry through the entire event. The passport would be signed and stamped at each checkpoint by the volunteer that manned it when the team passed through. If all the CPs were visited in the proper order within the thirty-six-hour time limit, a team would have an official finish. With my girlfriend, Kathleen, acting as our support crew, we had a team and were ready to go.

It was my first adventure race and, although I didn't know it at the time, I was about to enter a sport that would go on to consume the next eight years of my life. The first hurdle had been cleared and the four-person team was assembled, but we had many more unexpected challenges to go. My longest race to date had been around ninety minutes and now we were jumping into something that could last nearly a day and a half! In my youthful naiveté, I had no concept of what it would feel like to keep moving for thirty-six hours. In hindsight, this was probably a good thing.

On Friday afternoon we arrived at the race headquarters, located at Esprit Whitewater Rafting camp on the mighty Ottawa River, home to some of the best and biggest whitewater paddling in North America. Derek, Kathleen, and I had driven up in my 1989 Toyota 4Runner, one of the true loves of my life. Our teammates had driven in from Ottawa and we met for the first time after a month of communicating via email and phone calls. After taking some time for proper introductions, we dove into the gear check, which, as you'll discover in the next chapter, did not go smoothly.

On race day, we woke early to board one of several school buses that had been brought in for the occasion to transport the racers to the secret start line. This, we would learn, was a classic adventure-racing occurrence: the race directors would drive the athletes around, sometimes aimlessly, just to get them disoriented and add the extra element of fatigue before the event. In this case, the drive to the start was slower than anticipated due to the bus convoy getting lost—not a good omen before our first race!

We stood nervously on the starting line with thirty-three other teams. Kathleen was there, excited for us to begin our adventure. I couldn't help but notice that most other teams had two support members and many of the teams that we had spoken with seemed to know what they were doing. I really felt like a fish out of water despite the fact that I had grown up camping, hiking, paddling, and riding. This was definitely new territory for me and I was nervous.

The race began at 9:10 a.m. with race director Dave Zietsma simply yelling "Go" after a quiet countdown. The mass of racers began to surge down the dirt road we were on. Some ran, while others walked. We did a run-walk while Derek began describing our route. What made the start interesting was that not all the teams headed off in the same direction, with some beelining off on their own into the bush. Since it was our first event, this left us scratching our heads a bit, but one of the tidbits of advice that Dave had shared with us the night before was to race our own race. "Don't worry about what decisions other teams are making," he said, "because, frankly, they could be wrong." With those words echoing in our heads, we continued on our planned route.

Despite substandard gear and various mishaps, the

team soldiered from checkpoint to checkpoint until we finally crossed the finish line just under the thirty six hour cutoff. We were amazed that the faster teams had finished over ten hours earlier, but we were happy with our accomplishment and proud of the grit each person had shown—including Kathleen, as we learned that supporting a four-person team is not a one-person job! Most important, a team of young newbies had succeeded on pure guts and determination. More experienced teams had dropped out, but despite the challenge, we had never even considered giving up as an option.

I had found my sport, and completely immersed myself in it over the next eight years, competing with Derek in thirty-six-hour to five-day-long races across North America and beyond. I was still making mistakes but fewer of them now than I had in the past. I never really minded making these errors, just so long as I learned from them. I was starting to figure out the sport and was creating rules for myself to follow to help ensure success. The life I am living today is the result of that decision I made in 1998. I am so glad I let Pete talk me into taking the big leap of my first race.

One of the greatest realizations that I've taken away from adventure racing and applied toward all other aspects of my life is the importance of taking on big challenges that seem impossible at the time. This mentality has led me into areas in my life that I had little knowledge about before, and it is what led me to start my oatmeal company, Stoked Oats. If I had listened to doubt, my fear of failure, or my fear of success, I never would have started the company. The same is true of *Boundless* and Adventure Science. I've learned that the most important part of starting something new is making the personal commitment to give it your best shot—whatever that may look like. Failure isn't death; failure is learning, so I view each new challenge as an opportunity to learn and hopefully improve for the future.

Be Specific

Some of the best advice I've ever received about training came from Race Across America record holder Kevin Wallace. When I asked him how I could get faster on my bike, he answered, "Ride your bike more." If you want to improve at a particular sport, focus your training on it exclusively. That's it, pure and simple. The greatest athletic success that I've ever achieved (running or cycling) came when I trained specifically for goal races in a single sport. *Boundless*, unfortunately, requires us to be a jack-of-all-trades, master of none—which means that in any given season, we need to train for a handful of different sports, never achieving mastery in any. Sure, we all come into it with our strengths, but even those diminish as we spread our training time over a multitude of events. If you want to achieve your maximum potential as an endurance athlete, the only option is to specialize in your sport of choice and give it your all.

3.

Light Is Fast

I'm definitely a pack rat, often forming sentimental attachments to inconsequential objects and things. It's a trait that I am conscious of and try to mitigate. I don't want to accumulate stuff—because stuff bogs you down and can prevent you from following your dreams and ideas. Being acutely aware of this, I also apply this light-and-fast mentality to my expeditions, races, and even business, as bulk and bloat will slow anyone down, regardless of how strong you are or what momentum you have.

I learned this lesson the hard way in my very first race. As I mentioned in the previous chapter, all teams are required to carry mandatory personal gear and mandatory team gear. When I received a list of mandatory gear beforehand from the organizers of Raid the North, I really had no idea what most of the items were, as I was a mountain biker at the time who had never encountered these kinds of requirements. I wasn't even sure what shoes to wear! Believe it or not, I actually initially considered using my soccer cleats for the race, as I thought that hiking boots would be too heavy once waterlogged. Thankfully, one of my cycling buddies sold me on something called an approach shoe, which was popular with climbers and used to basically walk from the car to the crag. It is not as beefy as a hiking boot but more substantial than a conventional running shoe, so it seemed like a good choice that would be light, tacky, useful for light climbing, and capable of drying quickly.

Considering my limited student budget, I didn't have the money to buy much additional gear for the event beyond some fancy shoes, so I was forced to borrow and upcycle most of it. For my backpack, which I would quickly realize was one of my most important pieces of gear, I settled for my nylon school bag with one central zipper and a small pouch on the back. I borrowed a pair of cotton bouldering pants from my best buddy, Greg, and bought some hiking socks, as well as a long-sleeved polyester shirt. Since I'd only ever owned flashlights, for the headlamp requirement I settled on a clunky but cutting-edge Petzl zoom headlamp, which more closely resembled a coal miner's lantern then a sleek and powerful modern light. Regardless, it was a far cry from the bulky handheld six volt I used while camping. I was new to this and was excited to learn about this world of gear and technical equipment.

The other supply I needed to get in advance was food. Nutrition was definitely an area that I had limited experience in at the time. Powerbars had just hit the market and we were eating them like crazy when we were riding, but beyond that I had no clue what to pack for a race this long. Pete had told me that when Dave raced Eco-Challenge, all he ate, outside of the provisions at transition areas, was candy—gummy bears to be precise, chosen because they gave him instant energy and were palatable. I was skeptical, but I took Pete's advice and headed to the local grocery store, where I picked up two 1 kg containers of gummy bears for in-race food. For the transition areas, we were planning on soup, peanut butter and jam sandwiches, and maybe some pasta. We were going to use Gatorade to replenish our electrolytes, and we'd keep water on hand to fill bladders and bottles, as well as a few cans of Coke for a caffeine boost late at night. All in all, pretty low tech.

These are the things I brought to gear check with my fingers crossed. Our team moved through the gear list without too much trouble, though I had guessed wrong about two items. (It is worth noting that, in 1998, we didn't have the ease of hopping online and Googling something to find out what it was.) The first was the emergency blanket, which I had never heard of prior to this event. An emergency blanket is not, as I learned in embarrassing fashion, the wool blanket that I had brought, but some tinfoil, space-age ground sheet designed to reflect your body heat back on you, to keep you warm in an emergency. Go figure. My second, and most interesting, oversight had to do with the requirement that all athletes bring a fixed—or locking—blade knife. Being the ingenious young fellow that I was, I had brought a retractable X-ACTO knife. The volunteer running the gear check did not pass my knife, even though it had a locking mechanism. (As it turns out, I was ahead of my time; today, most athletes race with lightweight X-ACTO knives.) Because my team was now down a knife, we risked not being able to race, since we could not complete our gear check. Thankfully, a Toronto firefighter named Mano Krueger, who was one of Dave's teammates, had a spare fixed-blade knife to loan me. I was grateful to be back in the race but also a bit speechless, as the knife he gave me was an eight-inch-long commando knife that strapped to your calf. I felt like Rambo when I had that thing on.

We passed gear check after all, but our issues with less-than-ideal gear were far from over. The race began.

It was late morning and our race was going as well as could be expected, but some of my equipment decisions were catching up with me. As part of our mandatory team gear, we had to bring a shovel for human waste. Instead of going for a spoon or plastic garden spatula, which all the other teams had brought (I somehow missed that memo), I opted for a metal folding shovel—a military-style one that was overkill in every possible way, including weight. We were also required to bring duct tape, one of my favorite tools in the world. Instead of taking a small length and winding it around another mandatory item, such as a pen, knife, or other cylindrical object, I went for an entire roll. My race food, as per Pete's advice, was a 1 kg container of gummy bears still in their original plastic container. Apparently, the weight of these items, plus that of the other mandatory gear (excluding, of course my Rambo knife, as that was strapped firmly to my calf), was more than my backpack could handle. It ruptured during this first trekking leg. What made it funny was that just moments before, I had been complaining about my heavy, uncomfortable pack, and Derek had been quick to chastise me on my packing decisions. When the pack tore apart, though, it was my family-sized roll of duct tape that saved the day. Now, would the pack have torn without the extra weight of the duct tape? Probably, in my opinion. Regardless, it was the duct tape that saved the day. Derek and I still disagree but laugh about that moment to this day. When I think about this simple pack compared with my high-tech Camelbak packs that I use today, I can only shake my head.

As I competed in more races, I homed in on a nutrition strategy that worked, and pared down the weight of my mandatory gear. I learned my lesson about the benefits of carrying very little. Gone were the military folding shovel, the family-sized roll of duct tape, the kilo of gummy bears. In many respects, my pendulum for packing light swung to the other extreme—with my new goal being to always go as light as possible, or at least as light as I could financially afford (with gear, less is more—dollars, that is!). This, interestingly enough, brought with it new challenges and limitations. For example, when you pack light, you'd better be traveling fast because setting up bivies (temporary shelters in which to wait for rescue, etc.), longer than anticipated treks, and unexpected bad weather can be very character building, to say the least! Less gear often meant being colder and hungrier. It seemed that in order to go faster, I would have to get mentally tougher.

This lesson was brought to the fore during the second *Boundless* episode of season one when we traveled to central Iceland to compete in the inaugural edition of the Fire and Ice Ultra, a 250 km running race that took us from the Vatnajökull Glacier (Europe's largest glacier) northward to the coast. The race promised to be a visual masterpiece, as we'd run through denuded glacial terrain, along sand dunes, past raging rivers and towering waterfalls, and even through forests, which are a rarity on the island. This type of race was completely new territory for us.

Fuel the Engine

To finish ultras, you need three things: physical stamina, mental toughness, and good nutrition (including electrolytes). Over my decades of racing I've tried a lot of different nutrition strategies to help get me to the finish line. During this time, my tastes have changed as well. Gone are the days when my race diet consisted of bars and gels. While I still keep those on hand for emergencies, I've now transitioned to using more real foods because I find these much more palatable. Importantly, these are things that I look forward to eating. You never want to pack a bunch of food in your pack that you don't want to eat, because you just won't be able to stand them twelve hours into a race. While some of this is experience gained through trial and error, you can refine your nutrition strategy for races by testing out various foods in your training ahead of time. Most experienced endurance athletes take calories every forty-five minutes to an hour. Depending on the intensity of your effort, certain foods will go down easier than others. If you're going to be pushing hard, liquid calories have a lot of value, but carrying excess hydration is heavy, so that's always a consideration. I once tested this strategy when I raced the Chuckanut 50K in Washington State. To save weight, I decided not to carry any water, relying only on the aid stations to keep me hydrated. Over the course of the event, I drank about half a liter of water and had one gel. My science experiment yielded the following result: thirty-fifth overall, 4:30 time. I bonked hard during the final ten kilometers of the run, walking part of it and watching my goal of finishing in under four hours slip away. I learned the hard lesson that nutrition should be experimented with only during training, not in races.

With Turbo and me still reeling from the beating we had endured on the Channel of Bones in Hawaii, we made sure that we were adequately prepared to tackle this challenge. We dove into researching stage races and sought out mentorship from the best stage racers we knew in order to get their tips. These happened to be Ray Zahab, Mark Tamminga, and Joany Verschuuren. One of the constant messages was to go as light as possible, as we'd be carrying everything we required for the race on our backs, daily, except for our tents and water refills. Turbo and I got busy finding the lightest sleeping mats, ultralight clothing, the smallest lights, and more. Gear and clothing, however, only constituted part of it, as our food was the bulkiest item in our bags at the start of the race. In order to minimize weight, we both trimmed our race food to a mere 2,800 calories per day (we'd be running approximately a marathon a day for seven days straight), which meant we'd certainly be racing at a major caloric deficit. Based on exercise studies that I have participated in, I know that, at 60 percent of my maximal effort, I burn around 550 calories per hour. At race pace, I crank effort toward my aerobic threshold at around 80 percent. I can expect to burn approximately 800–900 calories per hour, which on a four-hour stage will amount to roughly 3,200–3,600 calories. Simply racing for four hours per day would leave me with a deficit of approximately 400–800 calories, and that's before you factor in the energy that your body requires to walk, talk, breathe, and even sleep. I went into this race figuring that I'd be hungry and weak by the end of it, but I really had no concept of how my body would react to this starvation diet.

On the starting line of the first stage I looked around and was amazed by the variety in pack sizes that I saw, with many athletes carrying what looked to be forty-pound packs. They must have had several outfits and unlimited food in there. I wondered if we had made a mistake. After the first stage, however, I knew that we hadn't, as Turbo and I finished first and second respectively; my winning time for that rugged 42 km stage was 3:45. My pack didn't seem to bother me and the weight felt evenly distributed. I was happy—that is, until it was time to sleep that night.

The forecast for late August 2012 was for daytime highs of 15 to 20°C (59 to 68° F) and nighttime lows of 5°C (41°F). Unfortunately for us, a cold front settled over us for the duration of the race—dropping the lows to -10°C (14°F) and daytime highs in the -5 to +5°C (23 to 41°F) range, until the final two days. Couple that with a relentless wind, and each day was as much a battle against the weather as it was against the route. We'd finish a stage and immediately get into our tents for warmth, which was hard to come by with all of our ultralight gear and minimal food. When the body is cold, it cranks its engine up, which ramps the metabolism. The result is a greater consumption of calories, which is why you are usually famished when you come in from exercising on a cold day, because your body is working not only to feed your muscles but also to keep your body warm in the cold conditions, which is more energy-intensive than trying to stay cool on a hot day. Our caloric deficit just got deeper.

That week was both a wonderful experience, as the beauty of Iceland is beyond words, and one of the coldest and mentally toughest that I have experienced on a race course. We learned in that race the importance of being nimble with respect to moving quickly, but we definitely paid the price for that strategy when we were forced to suffer through unseasonably cold weather.

I take the same approach with Adventure Science. I purposefully keep the teams small so that they can be both manageable and maneuverable should circumstances arise that require some major adaptation. I was reminded of this in Madagascar several years ago when I led a project to search for caves, dinosaur tracks, archaeological sites, and lemurs in the remote and foreboding Tsingy de Bemaraha National Park. We had stepped into the big leagues, acquiring sponsors, travel support, and a structured communication plan. Basically, we now had deliverables for our sponsors and supporters.

Due to the area's impossibly rugged and remote nature, the poor conditions of the few existing roads, and the permits required to conduct scientific surveys in that part of the park, my usual team of four to six members ballooned to over twenty. We had gendarmes, cooks, park rangers, two media managers, two drivers, and several local Malagasy men whom we had hired to do odd jobs like cutting trails or fixing or building so-called roads. To put this in perspective, the 800 km drive from the capital city of Antsalova was a three-day affair, as the Land Cruisers were reduced to a crawl over badly eroded roads and cattle tracks.

While the project was successful, the overall management of it was orders of magnitude more complicated than the typical project, and we were much slower-moving due to the size and scale of everything. I was responsible for my people and all the moving parts, and I quickly realized that each group had its own expectations of the project. My athletes wanted to be in the forest exploring from sunrise to sunset and going hard. The goals of the communications team I brought differed from those of the athletes, which created friction and strain within the team as they struggled to get the live media content they desired. The local Malagasy rangers we paid to accompany us were unaccustomed to our style of light and fast travel and required significant additional resources, as well as convincing and cajoling, to explore regions of the park they had never visited. Uncharacteristically for these projects, much of my time was spent managing the different components rather than focusing purely on the science and exploration. Lesson learned—I traveled with a large and cumbersome team and tried to serve too many masters, in the process losing focus to some degree on why we were there in the first place. I lost the feeling of being nimble and reactive, which I regretted and vowed never to repeat.

Stoked Oats also follows a very similar light-and-nimble philosophy. We have designed our company in such a way that we let true industry experts handle business in their area of expertise, and we manage the components to ensure that they all maintain our vision and direction. We don't operate out of a central office or have a lot of fixed overhead costs. Structuring our business this way has allowed for rapid growth and low overhead and operational costs. There may be a time when we have to adjust this model to adapt to the needs of a growing company, but in these early stages, being nimble and reactive has been the most important characteristic of our success.

In life, I like to feel light and move quickly—be it on the race course, during an Adventure Science project, or in business. I don't like the encumbrances that "attachments" can bring. Although I do value relationships, I try to avoid *baggage*, both emotional and otherwise, as ultimately it crushes our freedom and reduces our ability to adapt or to take the best course of action at any given time. Maintaining a light and fast condition is not always possible, but it is my ideal, and I evaluate all of my opportunities in that way.

4.

Embrace the What-If and the Unknown

Life changes drastically and suddenly when the gun goes off, but it's during the final moments preceding the race that I deal with the most anxiety. It's in these final moments that my blood really gets pumping. The training and prep are done and I always find myself in the what-if zone: What if this race is too hard for me? What if I didn't train hard enough? What if we get smoked out here . . . ? Once the gun goes off, though, I focus and get down to business. All the pre-race worries melt away.

The what-ifs can drive you crazy if you let them, or you can choose to embrace the unknown and adapt to whatever comes your way during a race and during life itself. One of the aspects of adventure racing that I loved the most was how it often put us in fish-out-of-water situations, forcing us to adapt or learn a new skill to prepare for the event.

The 2001 Eco-Challenge presented my team (Jeff MacInnis, Scott Ford, and Trisha Westman, at that time) with an unexpected challenge at the start line that required us to adapt, and quickly. For this race, which took place on New Zealand's South Island, all the competitors rode school buses along a bumpy country track for several kilometers to reach the start line. We disembarked at the edge of a long fence; each of the rails was a tall flag, each displaying a different nationality. Tethered to the fence posts were 134 horses, two for each four-member team. Each horse could only carry one person, which meant that two people from each team would have to run while the other two rode. I didn't know much about horseback riding—I hadn't grown up doing it and had spent minimal time working on the skill. Because Jeff had seen something like this in the previous year's Eco-Challenge in Borneo, he had a feeling that the race organizers would throw a twist at us at some point on the ride, so he suggested that he and Scott start on the horses, while Trish and I ran beside them. He reasoned that the athletes who rode first would be required to trek through one of the mountains in the distance while the two on the ground would then have to ride. It was a hunch, but we went with it and, since he was the navigator and Scott our best runner, it made sense that they ride first. We hurriedly saddled and bridled the horses, adjusted the stirrup lengths, and basically made sure that the animals were good to go for when the gun went off.

My neck was tight, as the pre-race nerves had put it in spasms that morning while we dismantled our camp and prepared for the start. As the clock ticked down, though, I was too preoccupied to really pay it much attention, although the sudden relief might have been due to the four vitamin I (ibuprofen) pills I swallowed to numb the pain. The scene was chaotic, with many horses already choosing not to cooperate with their assigned teams. Even our reasonably well-behaved horses showed their stress when one kicked the other for no particular reason. With the race start imminent, we assumed our positions. Scott and Jeff were perched on their steeds, while Trish and I stood near the horses' heads, with the reins in hand. We had decided that we would jog beside the horses, holding the reins to ensure they didn't buck or bolt.

Suddenly, Mark Burnett's voice cut through the air, silencing all except the braying horses. Over his megaphone he counted the race down from 5, 4, 3, 2, 1, and then he pulled the trigger of the starter's pistol held high above his head. *BANG*. My Olympics had just begun.

I don't know whether it was the gunshot or the surge of athletes that bothered the beasts most, but whatever the cause, a scene of pandemonium played out on that lonely pasture as horses threw riders and athletes scrambled out of the way of sprinting animals. Meanwhile, we moved at a steady tempo, Trish and I each leading a horse. The rules were that all members of the team had to stay together and that the horses couldn't go faster than a canter, which is faster than a trot but slower than a gallop. We ran like this to the first passport control (PC) at the 7 km mark without any issues, despite the challenge of running over tussock grass. Miraculously my shoulder and neck had improved, and the only drama during the first seven kilometers was when my horse stepped on my foot. Perhaps it was the soft grass we were running on, but I escaped with merely a bruise, having dodged a potentially race-ending bullet. We were easily in the front half of the field and feeling good. The butterflies had left my stomach and I was focused entirely on the race and my responsibilities.

As Jeff had suspected, the race organizers threw a curve ball at us at this PC. Teams were told to split up. The people on horseback had to dismount and run a 10 km mountain leg, while the runners were to mount the horses and follow a trail around the base of the same small mountain. If all went well, the two halves of the team would meet on the other side at another PC, where we'd all proceed on foot into the first trekking leg of the race.

Scott and Jeff bounded off toward the mountaintop while Trish and I set out on horseback. For the toughest race in the world, things were going very well. We had been riding for an hour when the trail meandered toward a small stream. The sight of water prompted Trish to ask me if we could stop.

"I think my horse is thirsty," she said.

"It's fine, Trish," I replied curtly. "Your horse is not thirsty." No sooner had the words left my mouth than I felt guilty for being mean, so I changed my mind and said, "Okay, Trish, we can give our horses a quick drink, but then we have to keep moving."

We dismounted our horses and led them toward the edge of the stream for their drink. Much to Trish's dismay, neither horse was interested in drinking. After waiting for a few uneventful minutes, we tried to get moving again. Grabbing the pommel of the saddle, I put my right foot into the stirrup and swung my left leg up over the horse, and then I turned to watch Trish attempt to do the same. What followed might as well have been a comedy routine, as Trish tried, unsuccessfully, to get up on her mount. Each time she went to swing her leg up to mount the horse, the animal would spin toward her, preventing her from getting up. This scenario repeated itself numerous times before I finally had to dismount and intervene by trying to hold the horse steady, which was easier said than done. Of course, now that the horse was delaying us with his antics, I was annoyed at myself for feeling guilty enough to stop. With Trish finally back on the horse, we resumed our forward progress.

They say that horses can tell when their riders lack confidence. If that is true, my horse must have thought that I was a joke, because I had zero confidence in my riding ability. The ride, for the most part, went pretty smoothly, although I learned a few things about my horse's personality, including (1) she must be in front of any pack of horses, and (2) she was prone to random sprints. It was one of these random sprints that could have been a race ender. For a reason I can't now remember, if indeed there ever was one, my horse suddenly began galloping, leaving me hunched over and clinging to the animal as it raced directly toward a hard bend in the trail, which then dropped sharply for about ten meters to the rock-strewn creek below. I somehow managed to stop the beast but not before it gave me the scare of a lifetime and a strong reminder that, in these races, it's never the fast downhill biking or the treacherous mountain traverses that will get you, but the what-ifs. In this case it was being an inexperienced rider on an unfamiliar animal in rugged and unforgiving terrain. It was about making decisions and dealing with the consequences. It's a trend I've seen repeated time and time again in racing, business, and life. Just when you think you've got it all figured out, life throws a curveball and all you can do is take your best swing at it and hope you make contact.

Our Adventure Science team frequently met the challenge of adapting to circumstances outside of our control.

Enter the Dragon

Even after filming two seasons of *Boundless*, I was nervous about appearing on CBC's *Dragons' Den*, a television show on which entrepreneurs pitch their businesses to a panel of investors with the cameras rolling the entire time. Watched by over one million households weekly, *Dragons' Den* could boost your business substantially if you made a good impression, but if you blew it, you could crater your company. When Stoked Oats was invited to participate, my team and I had long conversations about how to best position and present ourselves strategically. One piece of advice from our mentors was to use our appearance on the show purely as a marketing opportunity. To create drama and guarantee airtime, we could ask for an exorbitant amount. We needed investment, but we weren't in a do-or-die position. However, asking for too much would likely bring the ire of the Dragons and make us look naïve at best or greedy at worst. We didn't like either of those outcomes so we went in with a fair evaluation. After forty-five minutes of questions (cut to seven minutes for television), we walked out with a deal. We took a big risk with our brand and thankfully it paid off. I credit this to having a superior product with a great brand presence, knowing all of the answers to financial questions, and going in with a reasonable business valuation. We face uncertainty as soon as we get out of bed every morning—being well prepared and making rational decisions help to mitigate what you can't control.

The expedition to Oman in 2011 taught us again and again the importance of being flexible.

Ever since completing my dissertation research on the region, I had felt an insatiable draw to return and explore more of the vast and beautiful sultanate. A rich history melded with a friendly people, an interesting culture, and spectacular scenery make Oman a true jewel in the Middle East. What drew me to the Musandam Peninsula, located in the extreme north of the Oman, was its geographic location. Soaring mountains and an absence of roads, towns, and presumably people made this a region ripe for exploration. The last research party to document its visit to this region was that of geologist N. L. Falcon, sponsored by the Royal Geographical Society of London in 1971. This survey produced several short reports on the region, but it was one sentence in particular, written by the project archaeologist, that captured my attention: "We were told of archaeological sites in the interior, but the terrain was far too mountainous to explore; therefore we did not visit them." If I had ever heard a challenge for Adventure Science to conduct field exploration, that was it; Falcon had unknowingly thrown the gauntlet down over forty years earlier.

My three field seasons exploring the lagoons of Oman for tsunami deposits had made me intimately familiar with the country. As far as Middle Eastern nations go, Oman is very progressive. Sultan Qaboos bin Said al Said, who wrested the nation from his father during a bloodless coup in 1969, is judged by most as a fair ruler who has provided for his people. Considering that at the time of the coup, sunglasses were banned and only five kilometers of paved roads existed in the entire country, huge leaps toward modernity have been made during the last forty years. Today, fast cars race along Chinese-built highways, posh resorts dot the coast, and schooling and health care are provided for all. These developments have been funded primarily by oil and natural gas reserves that are modest by Saudi standards; these fossil fuels provide enough wealth to keep the population content and pacified.

Unfortunately, not even Oman was immune to the ongoing Middle Eastern reforms that brought violence to many nations. Six days before we were to depart for Oman, the town of Sohar, located in the north, erupted in protest and violence. Thankfully, my expat friend in Muscat, Dr. Barry Jupp, assured us that the trouble was localized and that we should proceed with the trip anyway. Our team— composed of archaeologist Dr. Richard Rothaus, Adventure Science athlete/engineer Jim Mandelli, and me—decided over a conference call two days before departure that the situation seemed under control and that the politics at work in Sohar were probably nonexistent in the Musandam.

Khasab was our starting point. Located literally at the end of the road, this lively town is the jumping-off spot for all trips into the peninsula. Its proximity to Dubai and promotion of dhow cruises and diving charters draw a reasonable number of tourists to the region. Richard and I had identified several prospective areas for research along the coast and in the apparent highlands. From these targets, I had designed the expedition to begin on the northeastern tip of the peninsula and then work its way south back to Khasab. The first location that we were to visit was one that I had termed the "Machu Picchu of Oman."

Our plan was to drop water at predesignated campsites, which would be our base of operations for several days before we moved to the next one. We had our rations—approximately 2,500 calories per day of freeze-dried food and energy bars per man (which would put us at a caloric deficit). We had our tents, our 50 liter packs for major hikes, plus smaller day packs, and we had arranged for approximately 80 liters of water to be delivered to our hotel in 1.5 liter water bottles. Each man was rationed 3 liters per day for food preparation and drinking.

Although we'd done all the necessary planning and had our supplies, there is always room for things to go wrong in an expedition like this. We were pushing the limits of food and water in order to go light but ran the very real risk of running out of water. Daytime temps could easily reach 30°C (85°F) at this time of year. An injury could be fatal if we were unable to get help quickly. If an injury were to occur, our options were to activate our SPOT unit (a personal tracking device), try to place a cellular call, or send Jim or me overland to either Kumzar or Khasab to bring help, assuming that one of us was able to do so. What this did was reinforce the importance of vigilance and avoiding injury; even in the best rescue scenario, we were hours from medical help. The possibilities of water shortages and injuries were never far from our thoughts, but we were still optimistic because of our preparations and our ability to adapt.

During our first twenty-four hours in Oman, everything went as planned, despite our earlier scare about the violent protests. All the luggage arrived, we had a breakfast meeting with Barry, and then we caught our morning flight from Muscat to Khasab. In Khasab, our first priority was to hire a boat, the last step in our preparations. This was surprisingly easy. As we left the airport, we were intercepted by a young boat captain from Kumzar named Suleiman. He had a boat for rent and tried to ply the usual tourist trip—dhow cruise, snorkeling, dolphin watching, etc. Thankfully, he spoke some English and we spoke some Arabic, so we were able to explain our unusual request. Although he was very surprised by the nature of our trip, he said he could help us. After a quick negotiation, we arranged for him to pick us up at 6:30 a.m., agreeing on a price of 140 rials (approximately $350 Canadian) for what amounted to a one-day boat rental. He then drove us to a local hotel that had a vacancy and left us to prepare for the following morning.

With a boat secured, our greatest obstacle was removed and we were free to enjoy the rest of the day, although I couldn't shake the nagging feeling that, in a country like this, our luck, thus far, was way too good.

At ten that evening the other shoe did drop. The telephone in our hotel room rang, and the hotel concierge told us that we had a guest at the front desk who wished to speak with us. It was Suleiman. As the three of us descended to the ground floor to meet with our boat captain, tension filled the air. With the concierge acting as our translator, Suleiman told us in no uncertain terms that he could not take us where we wished to go after all. It was forbidden for a foreigner to travel there without an Omani guide because it is inside a military zone. He regretfully told us that our travel plans would be no good for us and no good for him. Just like that, we were without a boat captain and the project was in jeopardy. We needed to find a new boat—and fast. At best, we would lose a day. At worst, the trip would be canceled due to the military sensitivities of the region. The clock was ticking, and we couldn't do anything more until the morning, when I would have to enlist Barry's help.

By eleven the following morning, Barry had spoken to the environment minister and the commander of the naval base on Jazirat al Ghanim (Goat Island), both of whom instructed us to stay away and not trek the peninsula unless we had proper permission. "Permission? What the hell does that mean, Barry? How do we get permission?" I asked. He replied coolly, "I wouldn't worry about it. Just keep your head down, mate, and have a good trip." Keep our heads down?

Barry connected us with a tour company with a good reputation that had worked with his colleagues. We had nothing to lose. After a spirited session of negotiations, we found a new boat captain, arranged water drops, our drop-off, and a pickup option for our final day. We were back on track and had only lost one day, which wasn't awful. I had factored in a buffer day for something like this anyway, so we were still on schedule, though we were all moderately concerned about the military situation that we might encounter.

At 6:45 the next morning, I could feel the excitement in the air as the three of us watched our new boat captain, Mohmed Kumzari (an entertaining Kumzari native with terrific English), slowly maneuver his vessel to the rocky shoreline, where we had piled a mountain of gear, most of it food and water. It was a sweet relief as we finally pushed our fully loaded boat from shore. Soon, we sped northward alongside towering mountains that plunged steeply toward the sea. I stared at the magnificent sea cliffs and the craggy peaks they concealed and began to understand why this peninsula lacked roads.

In order to make this trip work, we would need fresh water. Based on our studies of the maps and the research we had conducted, we knew there was no guaranteed water on the peninsula. Kumzar was the only place we were certain was populated. Although it looked like small camps dotted the shoreline, we could not count on these for food or water when planning. We had toyed briefly with the idea of having a boat come every few days to bring water, but we doubted that this would work logistically, so we had opted to make all of our water drops in advance. That meant pre-packaging all food and supplies in rubberized, dry bags and hiding them in the wadis (dry channels) that we had selected as campsites. Although we had been initially skeptical about this plan, it worked surprisingly well. It ensured that we would have enough water to last us, provided we abided by our ration strategy of three liters per man per day, which, in a desert, was tight. If we failed to make our water drops, our health could be in serious jeopardy in such a hot and dry environment.

We spent the morning making four water drops at our preplanned campsites, and by noon, Mohmed's boat nosed onto a small beach that doubled as an occasional fishing camp. It was not a great place to camp, but it did have a flat spot located above high water, where we opted to stash gear while we hiked 200 meters up to check out a feature I had spotted on a satellite image and dubbed, rather hopefully, the "Machu Picchu of Oman."

There was no trail as we followed a steep wadi upward. The surface was a mix of grippy limestone and loose rubble. Numerous small caves appeared as we gained altitude; sporadic acacia trees provided some welcome shade. The steepness was taking its toll on our travel time. Our archaeologist, Richard, had come a tremendously far way in terms of improving his fitness for this trip, but in the heat he was struggling with the lack of trail and difficult terrain. I could see that our ambitious yet imperative schedule was in danger, as it became obvious that we wouldn't be able to hit as many spots per day if we traveled as a group. Fortunately, we had a few days at this location before any hard decisions would be required. For now, we could just soak in the fact that we were finally here.

As we crested the ridge, I could see a stone wall in the distance. It appeared to be the circular structure that I had first seen on Google Earth. It was approximately forty meters in diameter, with a central wall bisecting the structure. As it was very flat and sandy inside the ring, we made a team decision to move our camp there. This required Jim and me to return to the water, gather all packs and twenty-four 1.5 liter bottles of water, and hike back to camp. As we explored the immediate area, we discovered a deep cistern built into a natural fracture in the rock. The team was excited by this promising start.

We traveled several hundred meters uphill along the ridge, looking for the next prospect, which was the cluster of structures. What we found blew us away: more than twenty large, rectangular buildings, most with their walls still intact and the massive limestone lintels still perched above the doors. These had been built using large limestone slabs native to the location, with many weighing in excess of 200 pounds. It's not surprising that, although the roofs had collapsed on most structures, these robust buildings are still standing. Pottery shards littered the ground and helped give us a sense of when the site had been built, which we placed at at least the 1500s, but it was likely much older.

We explored the area and along the mountainous ridge over the next few days, finding more structures, several ancient trails, and a number of caves that had been walled off, possibly to be used as lookouts, since this area would have seen significant maritime traffic.

We awoke on day three to a fierce wind from the south that battered our tents and made it impossible to sleep (despite the earplugs). It was our planned departure day, so we were out of food and had only enough water to make it to our next campsite. For Jim and me, this meant a rugged and highly exposed 10–12 km walk along a

mountainous isthmus connecting us to the main peninsula—
at least an eight hour day crossing terrain of unknown difficulty. We had decided as a group that the terrain ahead
would be too difficult and dangerous for Richard to traverse
in order to reach the next camp so we had to consider our
options: we could either make a costly satellite phone call
for an expensive boat ride back to Khasab and endure a
week of boredom, or we could take a risk and scramble
down a steep slope to a small but active fishing camp 280
meters below our current location, to see if they could
transport Richard by boat to our next site. We had no idea
if the Kumzari fishermen would be friendly, but it was
worth the risk.

We stuck to our plan and, despite the winds, left our
camp by six in the morning to negotiate the tricky climb
down to the fishing camp. The route was steep and treacherous, with loose rock, vertical ledges, and thorny plants
slowing our descent as we cautiously picked our way
down with our heavy packs.

We reached the beach by 7:30 a.m. and definitely surprised the fifteen fishermen camped there. Thankfully they
were welcoming and, after a few minutes of negotiations, we were able to settle upon a price of 10 rials (plus
three cans of Pepsi) for Richard to be shuttled to our next
camp. The plan worked and our taking a risk paid off,
once again highlighting the need to be adaptable when

pushing limits, especially when everything you are doing involves forging new territory.

With Richard safely en route to our second camp location, Jim and I began our traverse across the jagged isthmus. What with the high winds and exposed ridge tops, our day was as exhausting mentally as it was physically. We gained and lost hundreds of meters at a time, and walked along narrow limestone ledges on ridgelines—it was certain death if we slipped. We encountered a number of archaeological sites, including walls, scattered pottery shards, and even crude lookouts built atop high points on ridges.

After nearly eight hours of walking, Jim and I hit the wall. Literally. We were cliffed out. After a day of scrambling on highly technical, shoe-destroying terrain, we had met our match. Two kilometers from our camp, a mountain peak rose over 500 meters above a fishermen's camp called Marwani. It had a vertical face and, from where Jim and I intersected it, it still towered nearly 200 meters above us. Physically and mentally drained, we evaluated our options—neither was good. We could risk a very dangerous climb to the top of the peak, or swallow our pride and scramble down the steep wadi to Marwani to again test the goodwill of the local fishermen.

As much as I hated to deviate from our plan, the climb down was really the logical choice. The risks of scrambling and free-climbing on tired legs were far too great. We backtracked several hundred meters, looking for a suitable wadi to enter. Unfortunately, we were in a very narrow point of the isthmus and the drops were steep, so we entered the main wadi above Marwani, dubbed "the Descent": 380 meters of terror on account of the loose boulders that occupied the upper 100 meters of the wadi and the two 30-meter-high waterfalls that had to be solved on our way down. We were spent and bloodied but grateful to be alive by the time we reached the beach.

We thoroughly surprised this group of fishermen, who were relaxing after a day on the water. After we convinced them that we were not soldiers, they were amazed to learn that we were trekking through the region. Generous and welcoming hosts, they served Jim and me sweet tea, apples, and oranges, which, after a day of eating energy bars, were a welcome treat. After our meal, we asked our hosts if they would help by ferrying us to our camp, where we could reunite with Richard. They obliged and then refused any payment. Truly hospitable people.

For the next four days, Jim and I rose early and scrambled 300–400 meters upward to the interior plateau to explore for archaeological sites and artifacts. Richard examined the coastal areas near where we camped for both tsunami deposits and archaeological sites. We compared notes in the evenings, discussing theories about the age of the sites, time of abandonment, etc. When it was time to move, we hiked to the nearest fishing camp and negotiated a ride. The only downside to this strategy was that we were unable to complete our expedition as initially planned and, in the end, hired a fisherman to shuttle us from the fishing village of Sharayah back to Khasab.

The Musandam Peninsula proved to be a worthy challenge. The terrain was rugged and the mountains were generally devoid of life, save the odd tree or goat. In this environment, without proper planning, one could easily die of thirst despite being within walking distance of small camps. As Falcon's 1971 report had suggested, the Musandam interior plateaus were indeed rich with archaeological sites. During our weeklong expedition, we discovered numerous villages, farming sites, cemeteries and graves, intact pottery, ancient tools, and even a German-made gin trap (a leg trap for large carnivores like caracals or Arabian leopards). Traversing the mountainous and steep terrain required extreme concentration and that took its toll, as each step had to be properly placed and each handhold tested before bearing any weight. Couple this effort with the calorie deficit we endured, and I was left feeling somewhat drained by the end of the week. While circumstance prevented us from seeing all that we had set out to see, we did accomplish a significant amount during the seven days and were the first researchers to accurately map and document the sites in the last forty years, if not longer. We proved that the peninsula is no place for the meek or those unable to adapt on the fly.

These expeditions are great teachers for me because they illustrate the importance of adapting a plan when faced with obstacles. This has been an invaluable lesson to take to heart in every situation, from relationships to racing to Stoked Oats. My personal outlook is that the only constant in life is change, and only those who adapt survive and thrive.

5.

You Are Only as Good as Your Team

For those of you who have watched *Boundless*, you'll know that Turbo (aka Paul Trebilcock) and I go way back as friends. When it comes to picking a teammate, I got lucky with him, as he is the yin to my yang in many ways. I first met Turbo in the fall of 2004 after finishing a local orienteering race near McMaster University in Hamilton. I had done well and was catching my breath when a guy in a ball cap and big sunglasses and sporting a six-inch goatee came up and congratulated me with such enthusiasm that I figured I must already know him— although I was at a loss to place him. As it turned out, that was just Turbo being Turbo. An exceedingly friendly person, he started training with our running group and was, at that time, the only ultrarunner I knew. We forged a great friendship over the years through racing, Adventure Science projects, and hanging out. When the opportunity to create *Boundless* came along, he was a natural pick for my partner. Through the three seasons we've certainly had our ups and downs on the race course but never in the friend-ship department. I wish all of my teams and relationships were that good!

Through the years I've come to realize that picking your teammates for group endeavors is both a science and an art, as the right team can take you to great heights, but the wrong team can bring you crashing down in an instant. No sport highlighted this better for me than adventure racing, where your fortunes depend as much on teamwork as they do on fitness and good navigation. During my years in the sport I was fortunate to race with many incredible teammates, but sometimes there was just too much intrateam friction to allow us to reach our full potential in these events.

Raid the North Extreme, in Corner Brook, Newfoundland, was both the best of races and the worst of races. It was the best because the race course was incredible, the weather was great, and we finished fourth in a very stacked field, behind only the top Eco-Challenge teams from the US, Sweden, and Spain. However, it was also the worst because we had a major team implosion, which created an open, festering wound that no amount of gauze or duct tape could repair.

I had first partnered with Jayme Frank and Sarah Vlug for Beast of the East. A couple based in Saint John, New Brunswick, they were successful adventure racers who were following a similar trajectory as I was and who had added some young muscle and firepower to more sea soned teams in the previous two years. They were quickly building a reputation as up-and-comers. During the two races prior to this race, we had achieved excellent results and worked reasonably well as a team, although there had been some arguments and it had become evident very quickly during these events that we were not a team of four all striking toward a common goal but two teams of two, working in a tenuous, albeit mostly symbiotic, relationship.

For the first two days of the Corner Brook race, the team was functioning as a single unit, and we were near the front of the field. While we felt pressure from the other teams behind us, the excitement of racing near some of the world's best spurred us on.

Two days into the race, I was starting to feel the effects of little sleep and a fast pace. We had dropped our mountain bikes at the second transition area in King's Point and quickly grabbed some food and drink before heading off at daybreak to the ropes sections, which would include a 100 m rope ascent up Corner Brook Falls, followed by a 17 km trek to a 100 m rappel down an unnamed waterfall. It was during this trek that the chinks in the armor started to show within our team. Jayme and Sarah were pushing the pace on the trek. We left the second transition area at a slow jog, but it was a pace I could not hold at the time so I asked if we could walk. The two of them walked ahead of us while Derek hung back with me to help me along. As we marched on, the gap between our duos grew. I could tell that Sarah was upset that I couldn't maintain the pace. She was hungry with ambition and wanted to catch the teams in front of us, but there was nothing I could do. That's another interesting part of adventure racing—due to lack of sleep, minimal food, and incredible mileage, we all hit the wall during the event but usually at different times. I was hitting the wall at a time when everyone else felt great, which slowed the team significantly. The best teams have fewer of these moments to deal with and can thus keep the overall pace much higher, but they are impossible to avoid entirely. What makes them the best teams, though, is that they know how to deal with these moments in a way that keeps the team together and moving forward at the fastest possible pace for the circumstances. They realize that the clock doesn't stop until all four members of the team cross the finish line, so there is no glory in racing ahead of your team—only ego. We might have been having a fast race at that point, but the way we were dealing with my slow-down wasn't how one of the world's best, seasoned teams would handle it. We were beginning to come unglued. Regardless, none of us were quitters so we soldiered on, with Jayme and Sarah leading the way and Derek and me working hard to keep them in view.

As the race wore on, the team tensions began to eat away at the glue that held us together. Sarah was the general most of the time—driving the pace and trying to push us all to move as fast as possible. I have to say, for someone around 5'6" tall, she had one hell of a fast trekking pace. Nothing major stood out aside from the fact that Jayme looked after Sarah, and Derek and I took care of each other—there was little crossover. If I got tired and needed a hand, I would ask Derek, and vice versa. If I needed to stop to do something, Derek would wait while Jayme and Sarah would push on. If Jayme or Sarah stopped, though, we all waited. I tried to ignore this and stay focused on the task at hand, which was to take care of my shit and move fast, but Jayme and Sarah's behavior had been the modus operandi throughout the entire race, and it was wearing on my nerves. Although we couldn't see it at the time, an invisible wedge was splitting the team apart.

We were all tired, both physically and mentally, having already covered several hundred kilometers. We were now pushing along on aching bodies with blister-covered feet. We were in "suck it up, princess" mode. Jayme, who had been handling the majority of navigating throughout the race, was feeling the effects of minimal sleep and asked for a quick fifteen-minute nap. It was the middle of the third day and I was wide awake—as was Derek, who was the secondary navigator. We were near what I thought was the top of a long, gradual hill in a part of the race known as the Topsails—a high, treeless plateau of undulating hills, bogs, shrubs, and several ancient and extinct volcanos rising hundreds of feet above the tundra. Without major landmarks, navigators relied purely on compass bearings, which, if incorrect, could lead teams significantly off course in this generally featureless tundra. Since neither Derek nor I were tired, I convinced Derek that we should quickly trek to the top of this hill to get a visual feature to navigate toward, so that when Jayme and Sarah woke up, we'd have some good news for them. We left Jayme and Sarah at a large boulder, a highly visible, truck-sized glacial erratic boulder midway up this ramp. (Glacial erratics are large pieces of bedrock that are often out of place in their present landscape due to the fact that they were picked up, often carried long distances, and then dropped by glaciers once they started to melt.)

Derek and I started trekking uphill, closing in on what I believed to be the top of the long ramp. As we approached it, though, we found to our dismay that it wasn't the top and that it rolled over to a lesser grade but continued to climb. Derek and I stopped to discuss the situation. "We need to go back," he said. "It's been nearly fifteen minutes and they will be waking up soon." I replied, "Jayme is exhausted right now and he needs the rest, so let's allow him to sleep a bit longer and get our answer." After a brief exchange, I once again convinced Derek and we forged ahead. By the time we had reached the true top of the hill and spotted the Gaff Topsail in the distance, nearly thirty minutes had passed. We took some quick mental notes and then hustled downhill and back toward Jayme and Sarah.

By the time we closed in on the large boulder where they had stopped to rest, nearly fifty minutes had passed. "Guys, we have some great news," I exclaimed from a distance. The reply chilled me: "Where the fuck have you guys been?!" Things immediately got worse as the pair of them verbally attacked Derek and me, calling us every name in the book for leaving them and accusing us of ruining our chances at catching third. We protested and tried to make our case, but it fell on deaf ears. The tension and animosity that had been building since the Beast of the East race several months earlier boiled over into a race-wrecking moment.

With the benefit of hindsight, I would have handled things differently. For starters, we had broken the 100 m separation rule, which technically could result in disqualification, but my biggest takeaway was that I should have stuck to the fifteen-minute curfew. I think my desire to help the team, gain some reassurance for myself, and possibly even have a hero moment overwhelmed my better judgment and Derek's. I was furious listening to the two of them tee off on Derek and me, but I took their criticisms of me because I knew I had fucked up and deserved it. I didn't feel that it was Derek's fault, though, and that's what got me angry. I put up a fight on his behalf.

Sarah was the first of the two to calm down; having said her piece, she was ready to get on with the race. Derek and I were more than happy to oblige. Jayme, on the other hand, shoved the map at Derek and said, "Here, I guess you're the navigator now." Derek and I were shell-shocked, but Derek accepted the map and we began moving again. We had lost an hour during that fifteen-minute stop. Live and learn, I suppose—at least we were racing again. Well, at least three of us were. Jayme had slowed his pace to a crawl, sulking and walking tens of meters behind the rest of us. We tried to urge him on, but he wasn't having any of it. I'm not sure if he felt that we had subverted his race or didn't have faith in his abilities. Maybe he was still furious about us climbing the hill. Whatever he felt, he was dragging ass until Sarah basically told him to "stop being a baby and pick up the pace," which he eventually did. The whole experience reinforced a key tenet in adventure racing—you are only as good as your team. Sarah and Jayme couldn't proceed without Derek and me when they woke up, and we couldn't make up time with Jayme dragging his butt.

A storm cloud followed our team from the Topsails to the finish line. Every exchange became very superficial. The strained chatter that we'd occasionally had during the earlier segments of the race vanished and we mostly traveled in silence. We spoke only as much as we needed to and basically raced as distinct duos for the remainder of the event. Derek and I tried to make the best of it and continued quietly, each of us reflecting on our own memories from the event as we closed in on Corner Brook.

It was sweet relief crossing the finish line in that remote Newfoundland town that we had left nearly one hundred hours earlier. The top four teams all finished within nine hours of each other, which made for a very competitive race. Our official finishing time was 96:50—a little over three hours behind third place, Team Red Bull/Playstation of Spain.

We had good luck in this race and rode the wave of great weather, and we also had bad luck with our team dynamics, which, admittedly, I inflamed through bad decision making. Regardless, we had made the podium, earned a paycheck for our efforts, and, most important, earned the respect and caught the attention of the greater adventure racing community in Canada (a fact I wouldn't be aware of until a month or so later). We were now a team to watch, and, at our young age, we were full of potential. It was also the last time Derek and I would race with Jayme and Sarah.

Our friend Hazen, who was part of our support crew and was responsible for transporting our gear and feeding us at transition areas during the race, had to get back to Saint John prior to the awards ceremony. As this was a huge victory for us, we all wanted to stay for the awards night and after-party. We discussed it as a team because Hazen was our only guaranteed ride back, and both Derek and I had flights to catch. As poor grad students, we didn't want to have to pay to change our flights.

Sarah and Jayme assured us that, since they knew so many people at the race who lived in the Maritimes, they'd be able to get us a ride back to the city. "Worst-case scenario," Sarah added, "my dad will drive up from Saint John and meet us at the ferry terminal in Cape Breton." So, with that assurance from our teammates, whom Derek and I had generally been avoiding since the finish, we sent Hazen off with our bikes and duffel bags, which were filled with very pungent and rotten gear.

The awards ceremony was a great party, but Derek and I, both still wheeled from the race, opted to turn in early. We chatted with Jayme and Sarah before heading back to the dorms. Although they hadn't found a ride yet, they were still optimistic about us finding one. I went to bed without a care in the world, sleeping soundly until I was jolted awake by a loud knock on my door. I got out of bed and opened the door, and was surprised at whom I found.

Standing at the entry in only his underwear was Derek. "Dude," he said, "they left us." He was holding a torn piece of foolscap with a handwritten note scribbled on it. It read: *Guys, we tried to find a ride back for all of us, but there was nothing. We found two spaces with some friends who are leaving tonight and are taking them. Good luck getting home and call us when you get back to Saint John.* I was livid. They had ditched us and we were the ones with flights to catch. More lessons learned.

What stung the most about this was not being left behind—because after this and a few of the previous races there was no love lost between the four of us—it was the promise that Jayme and Sarah had broken.

After regrouping over breakfast, we started chatting with other athletes and support crew members who weren't leaving until later in the day. We started looking at all of our options for getting to Saint John to pick up our gear and the check for our finish and to make our flights home—me to London, Ontario, and Derek to Berkeley, California. As luck would have it, we were able to talk ourselves onto a bus that took us to Channel-Port aux Basques and the ferry terminal—a short, two-hour drive from Corner Brook. Once aboard the ferry, Derek and I were able to find room in a van headed to Saint John. Our troubles were over. The elderly couple who owned the van had driven from their home near Saint John to volunteer for the race.

The most difficult part of the entire experience, race included, was not knocking Jayme out when I next saw him. I stood there, a boiling cauldron of rage, in total silence. Derek did the talking, I grabbed my money and gear, and then Hazen drove me to the airport. It took me a long time to forgive them for abandoning us like that, but ultimately time heals all wounds. For the next few years, Jayme and Sarah continued competing in races like the Adventure Racing World Championships, so they did get their chance to race against the big dogs. I had other opportunities come my way, and Derek became busy with work, life, and family and drifted from the sport.

With the benefit of hindsight and fifteen years to let my emotions simmer, I realize that there were things I could have done differently to better deal with Jayme and Sarah, but ultimately there are just some people with whom you gel and race well and others with whom you don't. The important thing is to be able to recognize people in the second category, to avoid partnering with them in sport or business.

As the 2001 Eco-Challenge approached, I had much better luck finding a team of people who worked well together. From our very first meeting, we laughed, shared war stories, and immediately connected, not only as like-minded athletes but as friends, too. They also took a chance on me, as I had torn my medial collateral ligament playing soccer a week before meeting them for my team interview. Their acceptance of me anyway was a gesture that was not lost on me. At the time, Scott Ford was a twenty-six-year-old open-water paddle specialist who came from a kayak racing background. He had raced with Pete Cameron in the past; because of this, I felt as though I already knew him. Pete, as I recall, even put in a good word for me with Scott. We hit it off immediately. In her early thirties, Yvonne Camus was a single mother of two twin boys. Unbeknownst to me, we had started our adventure racing careers at the same Raid the North race in Fort-Coulonge in 1998. What struck me about Yvonne was her bubbly and incredibly positive attitude. She was in fact so positive that, for the first few months that I knew her, I waited for the other shoe to drop, but it never did. She's probably one of the happiest people I know. Although I already knew a bit about the team captain, Jeff, from our initial phone calls, I was overwhelmed by how cool he was. Here was a guy living the life I dreamed about—basically, as a professional speaker who made his living talking about his incredible adventures. Here was a guy who, in his late thirties, had sailed the Northwest Passage, driven around the world, dove fantastic deep-sea wrecks with his world-famous explorer father, and been the subject of a cover story in *National Geographic*. Jeff became an instant mentor for me, and the mentorship has continued to this day. Suffice to say that the meet-up went well and, in short order, the team confirmed that I would be their fourth for the upcoming race. I couldn't believe my luck—I was going to the Eco-Challenge and would meet my goal of competing in the race by the time I was twenty-five.

The team received some bad news in the weeks leading up to the event. Yvonne would be unable to join us for that year's race due to her parenting responsibilities. She was crushed, and we found ourselves in the unenviable position of having to find a fast, experienced, and qualified female to join us for what Eco-Challenge was calling its "toughest race yet." In the days before Facebook and Google, that was a tall order, especially since we only had dial-up Internet! As luck would have it, though, I knew someone who might just fit the bill. I had met a young engineer named Trisha Westman nearly a year earlier when she and her adventure racing superstar boyfriend Lawrence Foster had come to the mountain bike center I managed at the London Ski Club. The three of us had become good friends. With Trisha living and working in London, she and I trained together regularly. She had also been on our winning team earlier that year at a very competitive thirty-six-hour race called the Adventure Racing Canada (ARC) Outback in Haliburton. Fit, fast, experienced, and well-qualified, Trisha was, in my opinion, one of the best-kept adventure racing secrets in Canada, if not in North America. My sales pitch to the team was well received and, before we knew it, Trisha was rolling with the squad. Like me, she'd had her eye on the Eco-Challenge for many years. I found this out before we left when she showed me a handmade card from her mom, which wished her the best of luck but also congratulated her on "her scheming" and that it had finally paid off. While I'm still not sure exactly what type of scheming she did to secure a spot on an Eco-Challenge–bound team, we had a good laugh about that one.

The best teams are successful in part because each athlete knows their role and accepts it. A team's overall physical prowess doesn't mean much if the members cannot work together as a unit, to help each other along. Thankfully, Scott, Jeff, Trish, and I all worked very well together, knew our roles, and accepted them. Although it's always important to have dialogue with respect to key decisions, there ultimately needs to be a captain who, while being open to other opinions and perspectives, calls the shots. Jeff was this person on our team. As the oldest team member and by far the most experienced adventurer, Jeff had secured sponsorship for the team and basically was the reason we were here in the first place. We all respected him as an athlete, navigator, and leader. He was in charge of the maps, consulting us when needed but otherwise making all the navigational calls. An exceptionally strong cyclist, Trish brought her own special flair to the team. Always upbeat, she was in charge of keeping us informed of the written instructions that had been provided by the race organizers to assist with navigation. She also had the added carrot of wanting to beat her Eco-Challenge veteran boyfriend, Lawrence, who was racing on Canadian team Subaru Outback, captained by Dave Zietsma. Scott was a solid jack-of-all-trades. Undoubtedly the best paddler on the team (and possibly in the race), he was also an incredibly fast runner and solid rock climber. His versatility extended to navigation, and he backed up Jeff on the maps when needed. Due to our youth, and perhaps due to my extra time in the gym that season, Scott and I were the designated mules of the team. Our job was to push hard and carry the most weight. Extra sleeping bags, crampons, and all mandatory team gear—those items went into our packs. While not a huge burden on the legs, the extra weight definitely manifested in throbbing feet and a mess of blisters after several days of racing.

The true test of a strong team is how it reacts to adversity, not success. New Zealand was a hard-fought success. Everything went well and we exceeded expectations. Unfortunately, Eco-Challenge Fiji in 2002 went awry from the start. We never quite found our rhythm in that race. No matter how hard we pushed, we just couldn't work our way to the front of the field. Tough navigation in the jungle slowed us, and a horrible foot rot that plagued most racers in the event eventually forced our withdrawal, with Trish getting airlifted from the base of a remote waterfall, and Jeff, Scott, and I hiring a priest at a local village to drive us several hours on rutted dirt roads into Suva so that we could catch a shuttle to the finish line. Despite this disappointing result, our friendship and teamwork never flagged. Those are the types of teammates you want in sport, and in life. The four of us are still friends to this day and still compete together occasionally or come together for Adventure Science projects.

Shortly after my Eco-Challenge New Zealand experience, my school newspaper, the *Western Gazette*, quoted me as saying, "You rely on your team. When you feel low, there is someone there to buoy you up. The communication has to be open—you've got to be able to tell somebody you hate their guts one minute and that you love them the next." In a race as tough as this, you're only as good as your team, so if you speak honestly, laugh often, and have a little fun while you're all pushing each other to your limits, you're probably going to succeed.

Blaze, one of Adventure Science's early projects, was another race that taught me a lot about teamwork. In 2009 I partnered with my friend, adventure racing teammate, and renowned medical doctor and exercise

People Are Always the Priority

In the spring of 2016 I returned to the Musandam of Oman to take another crack at completing the traverse that had stymied Jim, Richard, and me five years earlier. This time, armed with knowledge of the terrain and people of the region, I was sure we'd be able to complete the trek. I had assembled a team of very fit athletes, including Adventure Science veterans Jim Mandelli and Tim Puetz, and our photographer, Luis Moreira. New to the team was a good friend from Calgary named Myron Tetreault.

The trip was turning out to be an excellent one and we had made new and exciting discoveries, including that of an ancient mountaintop fortress that sat high and forgotten above the isolated village of Kumzar. We made our way south through the interior plateau, looking for ruined villages and farms, as well as for evidence of the critically endangered Arabian leopard, thought to be extinct in the region. After two days of walking south from Kumzar, the plateau began to narrow into a steep-sided and, in places, knife-edge ridgeline that ran around 450 meters above the ocean. The team was starting to feel the effects of nearly a week of trekking at this point, and fatigue was setting in. Part of going light each day meant that we didn't quite replace the calories that we burned through our efforts and, as such, were operating at a deficit and physically getting weaker the longer the trip lasted.

At one point, after the team had split up to investigate different things, I heard Myron shouting. I couldn't make out what he wanted and as he continued to shout to us, I began to fear that something serious had occurred. Once I got closer, I was finally able to understand the reason for the urgent yelling: Jim had stepped on a rock that broke free under his weight and he had fallen several feet onto his ankle, likely fracturing it. He couldn't walk. Just like that, the expedition's focus changed from exploring to mounting a rescue in a remote and rugged region with no roads, no cell coverage, and twenty kilometers between us and the town of Khasab.

I began to take stock of the situation and assign responsibilities. Tim, a wilderness-trained EMT, administered first aid. Myron put his background in swimming to use as he set off for the nearest fishing camp, about one kilometer away. Luis's job as the team photographer was to assist if asked but to otherwise record the moment with his camera, and I got on my iridium satellite phone with our emergency medical insurance provider to ensure that hospitals and transport were lined up so that there would be no lost time.

Myron soon reappeared perched atop a fishing boat with two Omani fishermen piloting it. Despite his lack of Arabic, he had managed to communicate the seriousness of our situation and need for help. As they had in 2011, the Omani fisherman had jumped to action.

I paused for a millisecond as we loaded Jim onto the boat and I realized that our expedition was over, but I didn't feel regret. We all set off for the port of Khasab, where an ambulance would be waiting for Jim. In moments like these, the big team objectives pale in comparison to the real-life emergency unfolding before you. We can always return to Oman to complete the traverse, but a delay in treating Jim's severe fracture could have resulted in further complications down the road, which is never worth risking for the sake of a project.

As a team, we had accepted the risk that the traverse posed and tried to mitigate it as well as we could, but when you are in a remote and challenging terrain, and moving with a fatiguing team, sometimes the worst-case scenario does occur. I always remind myself that the adventure, the discovery, and the challenge are never a good enough reason for me to push my friends outside of their comfort zone. On these expeditions and in our daily lives, it is the people we surround ourselves with that are important—not our accomplishments.

physiologist Mark Tarnopolsky to create Blaze, which was an end-to-end relay race between two ten-person teams stretching the entire length of the almost 900 km Bruce Trail. We'd start in the village of Tobermory and work our way south along the trail, hopefully reaching Queenston Heights, the official start to the trail. Along the way, all athletes would donate fluid samples so that Mark and his team would be able to track, in his lab, the muscle damage that was occurring in each of us. As this was at the beginning of the ultrarunning resurgence, little was known about muscle damage that occurs when humans tackle long distances. The research ultimately resulted in a scholarly article entitled "Oxidative Stress, Inflammation, and Muscle Soreness in an 894 km Relay Trail Run."

While the science definitely motivated Mark and me, neither one of us was prepared to solo it or try with a two-man team. Realizing that others would be less interested in the science, we opted to create a competition, creating two equally matched teams with some of the best trail runners we knew to battle each other and the course record in a nonstop relay format. The two teams, Team Mitochondria (led by Turbo) and Team Muscles (led by me) were named in honor of the charities Mark and I had selected, Mitochondrial Disease Foundation and Muscular Dystrophy Canada.

During the day, runners would go solo, but due to the added risk of injury during the dark hours, each team had to put two athletes out per leg from dusk to dawn. While I enjoyed it, night running seemed to be the hardest on both teams. Attrition due to ankles rolled at night started to gut both of the squads, but amazingly spirits remained high on both teams, and the race remained a close one, with both teams gaining and losing the lead in a seesaw battle that went through the first two days. As we approached Toronto, the race was still far too close to call, with both teams separated by less than an hour. Although it was a heated competition, outside of our respective legs we were able to relax and laugh with friends on both teams. It was a unique racing environment.

Spirits were high but legs were sore when we stopped in Hamilton. Mark Tamminga, one of the racers on Team Mitochondria, pulled me aside to talk about the race. The teams, at this point, were about an hour apart, with Muscles in the lead. Mark, being the gentleman racer that he is, suggested that we race hard until the last stage and then bring both teams in together—Tour de France–style—with no racing on the final stage. Being the competitive person I am, I couldn't give him a definite answer, opting instead to consider the suggestion over the next few hours, weighing the pros and cons. The only real con to finishing together was that whichever team was in the lead might have shaved a few more minutes off the current record, which we were already demolishing.

I realized the record was ours and those few minutes were meaningless in the big scheme of things. We were in the process of doing something incredible and, even better, doing it as a large group of friends. I realized, as Mark already had, that celebrating the teamwork and camaraderie that existed within that amazing group of people was the more important aspect of this project, not the fastest-known time record. Our goals would be achieved, and we'd end with everyone celebrating the achievement. I could stop worrying and start celebrating . . . kind of.

My love of redefining limits for myself and others has been with me for a long time. We ran as a group toward the culmination of something that we had all worked so hard for. As tired and sore as I was, and as much as I was looking forward to this being over, I also realized that projects like this gave us all purpose. We were focused and passionate. The daily trappings of life were meaningless out here. All that mattered was running, resting, and doing it again. We had fallen into a routine but ran through fatigue and pain for a higher purpose—each other. We found strength and mentorship in the team. While it was wonderful to set the record—which is still standing and, due to the logistical challenges of organizing such a large group, will likely go untouched for some time—I was reminded of the lesson that I learned during my adventure racing days: that sometimes what lifts us up and allows us to be our best is not going it alone for glory but sharing the experience with people who matter to you.

6.

Chart Your Own Course and Take Responsibility for the Direction You Choose

Once you have accepted the fact that life is not a linear path, and that we will face what-ifs and unknowns daily, navigating all of life's challenges—whether self-imposed or otherwise—becomes more palatable. Like it or not, we are all in charge of the map. We are all responsible for navigating our own lives.

In adventure racing, the role of the navigator is certainly the hardest on the team. In charge of the maps and route finding, navigators hold the fate of their teammates in their hands. A perfectly navigated section saves time, boosts morale, and often moves teams up the rankings. A navigation error can send teams sliding down the rankings and drop morale, or, even worse, wear the athletes out as they cover unnecessary kilometers. The thing with navigating, though, is that you only get better through practice, and the only way to practice race navigation is to race, and unfortunately, the only way to learn is to make mistakes. I've always expected a lot from my navigator, but I also understand the pressure and how easy it is to get off track, so I accept that when we race, we will usually have to deal with a few navigational bobbles. Accepting this as part of the race leaves me mostly unfazed, because in adventure racing we all get tired and sometimes make mistakes. No navigator intentionally tries to lead the team off course. The same, I find, is true in life and business. With Adventure Science and Stoked Oats, I've learned through making mistakes.

With Adventure Science, one of my early mistakes was not scooping up several other Adventure Science domain names, such as adventurescience.org. My oversight allowed a copycat organization to spring up in the US and benefit from our SEO. This now creates confusion for people trying to follow Adventure Science projects and will ultimately have to be dealt with as both organizations continue to grow. One mistake we made in the early days of Stoked Oats was introducing a product called Vegan Oats. After receiving a number of requests from our highly vocal vegan customers who wanted our oatmeal but without the whey protein (we've since formulated all of our oatmeal blends to be whey-free), I figured that there was a market for whey-free oatmeal, and ultimately there was. What there wasn't a market for was a product that branded the consumer—especially non-vegans—which is what Vegan Oats unintentionally did. Even after we decided to end this failed experiment and to blow that blend out at bargain prices, we still found that we could barely give it away, despite the fact that it was virtually identical to another blend of ours. Let's just say that I ate a lot of expired Vegan Oats the following year after making this mistake. As annoying as it was, I'm glad that I made it in the early days of Stoked Oats instead of now, when a mistake like that would cost the company a lot of money.

In my first adventure race, we learned an important lesson about taking responsibility for our navigation the hard way. We had been racing for over twenty-four hours when we had a navigation decision to make that Derek would later recall as one of his worst adventure racing moments. We had been mountain biking a series of ATV trails and rural roads around daybreak and had stopped at a checkpoint to chat with Mano Krueger, the course designer who loaned me the Rambo knife. After talking, we rode off in what turned out to be the wrong direction. Tom and Heather had been fading for the last few hours and were totally deflated when they learned that we had made a mistake and ridden five kilometers out of the way. When we recognized our mistake, it stung, but we turned around and slowly headed back. We once again bumped into Mano. The look on our faces must have said it all because he immediately said, "Sorry, guys. I wish I could

Protect Your Brand

In the fall of 2011, three years after I started Adventure Science, I received a call from a young adventurer from Montana who was starting up an organization that acted like a matchmaking service, connecting adventure travelers with researchers in need of data collection (snow from a mountaintop, water from a remote creek, etc.). He was interested in learning more about what we did with Adventure Science, as he was in the early stages of creating a citizen science organization. He chose the name Adventurers and Scientists for Conservation and the URL www.adventurescience.org. Being supportive of the concept, I didn't ask him to change the web address. Fast-forward five years and his organization has dropped its original name and replaced it with Adventure Scientists. This change, plus the website similarities to my adventurescience.com, have created innumerable headaches and many cases of mistaken identity. I'm now in the process of dealing with this messy situation, but it's one that costs time and money to fix, whereas a correction in the early days would have allowed me to avoid this situation entirely. I've learned from this mistake that when it comes to intellectual property, there is no gray area. The world of business shares many attributes with athletics, perhaps the most common being that everyone can be friends off the course, but during the race it's a serious competition where there *is* a winner and loser. I've learned that in life sometimes you really have to fight hard for what's yours, especially when it comes to your intellectual property.

have said something. It was really hard to stay silent and watch you go the wrong way." At that moment, Derek worked hard to subdue a violent rage, but I think that all of us, Derek included, realized that this was adventure racing: there are no freebies or handouts. You need to know where you are going at all times and take responsibility for your decisions. This race taught me a lot, but this was one of those lessons that transcends sport and is directly applicable to how we live our lives. We chart our own course and are also responsible for the decisions we make along the way and for knowing where we are at any given time on our path. In life, as in racing, this is easier said than done. For Derek, who had been doing a great job navigating, it was a disappointing but also embarrassing mistake to make on a relatively easy road section in front of the macho course designer. As we rode away from Mano the second time, Derek summed up his feelings by saying, "What a dick," and then he put it to bed.

I've taken the concept of adventure race navigation and applied it to many aspects of my life. Navigators in an adventure race typically have a lot of freedom to choose the routes that suit them or their team the best. They make strategic decisions and move forward decisively. I've always been one to act on my ideas, founding the Boler Mountain Bike Centre at the ski hill in my backyard when I was eighteen, the Canadian Adventure Racing Association when I was twenty-four, and later Adventure Science (2008), Stoked Oats (2011), and *Boundless* (2012).

When I decided to leave my job as a geologist in August 2012, it was a major transition, as you might expect, but I knew in my heart that it was the right move to make. The big question mark was on how I was going to feed myself. Stoked Oats wasn't making enough money to pay salaries at that time, so from September to December I would only have my *Boundless* salary to survive on, which definitely wasn't anywhere close to what a geologist made in Calgary at that time. I couldn't rely on *Boundless* being renewed, so I knew that I had to focus on growing Stoked Oats, as well as living within my means, since my income would now be more sporadic. I also started doing something which I've since made a regular part of my New Year ritual—I take stock of the past year with regard to everything from income to love. I plan out my year, set my goals and timelines, and then go for it.

Taking big risks has never been intimidating to me, but perhaps that's because I tend to be cautious before I step out from a place of comfort and safety and onto the ledge. When I left my job as a geologist, I sold my house and still worked for three-quarters of a year, so I had reasonable savings to tide me over if *Boundless* didn't get renewed. I also created a timeline for myself where I set goals for myself, Stoked Oats, and Adventure Science.

I accepted that getting these businesses off the ground and growing a brand wouldn't bo oaoy or faot, but I now had financial resources behind me to give it an honest shot. I also set a one-year deadline. If *Boundless* didn't renew, and I wasn't able to generate an income from either Stoked Oats or Adventure Science, then I would return to the oil and gas industry as a geologist, which was my great fallback.

Thankfully, *Boundless* was renewed for two additional seasons, which became a great source of income and allowed me to spend more time growing both Adventure Science and Stoked Oats into viable businesses.

In charting my own course, I also look toward an ultimate exit point. *Boundless*, while an incredible experience, is very hard on the body. Although Turbo is still racing at age fifty, I'm not sure that I will be able to avoid injury for another ten years to make it to his benchmark, nor am I sure that I would want to even if I could. I enjoy new challenges; when something becomes stale, I tend to move on.

Thanks to the financial support of *Boundless*, I'm now at a point where if I'm injured and unable to race, all is not lost—and I will still be able to make a living through Stoked Oats or Adventure Science. I hope I have many years of racing ahead of me still, but I do look forward to switching gears and focusing my efforts on new projects, such as starting a family and developing the family farm—a 1,000-acre

Long Trek ranch in Sheenboro, Quebec—into an Adventure Science training center.

I feel that everyone's situation in life is mostly a direct reflection of the action or inaction we take on a day-to-day basis. Change can be intimidating, but only you can chart a path to your own happiness. It's not always going to be a smooth road, as there will be bumps and challenges, but if you accept responsibility and ownership for your decisions, you will be more empowered to forge ahead despite setbacks or negative events. I've been able to hone these attributes through racing, and I apply them daily in my non-racing life.

7.

The Greatest Amount of Luck Is Found at the Front of the Pack

I always joke that you have to be good to be lucky, but I've noticed in sport that it pays to be near the front, as that's where the greatest amount of luck seems to be. The early birds get the good weather, the best boats, the best food at aid stations, the best footing on a muddy course, and so on. Middle-of-the-pack and back-of-the-pack teams often face shortages at aid stations, bottlenecks on narrow courses, and long waits at obstacles. I've always felt that, most of the time, it's better to go hard early on and risk an explosion than to ease into it and face log jams later in the race—*if* your goal is to be competitive. That mentality is something of a carryover from mountain bike racing, where it is full gas from the gun as everyone tries to get in front of the pack and enter the single track first, for the person who is at the front of the single track controls the pace.

We definitely found this to be the case while competing in the Raid the North Extreme adventure race in Corner

Brook, Newfoundland, in 2001. We were moving quickly and surprisingly near the front of the field when, after forty-eight hours of trekking, rowing, and mountain biking, we arrived at a small village called Middle Arm, the starting point for a 50 km sea kayaking leg on the open ocean. We hit the water midday and paddled hard to beat the darkness, Derek and I in one boat, our teammates Jayme and Sarah in the other. We were gliding well and enjoying the generally calm conditions. When we started the paddle, the winds were light and the waves small, but I'd never paddled in the ocean before and was having flashbacks to the north channel of Lake Huron, where we had narrowly avoided capsizing in a harrowing storm with twelve-foot breakers during a race the previous year. As we moved into the open water, the swells began to increase. These waves gave us little to worry about, as they were large but not breaking, so there was little risk of capsizing. What was nice about the swells was that, if timed right, a boat could surf the back side, saving us energy and giving us a free downhill ride. The longer we paddled, the more we improved and soon we became quite adept at surfing, getting the most out of our paddling. As the afternoon wore on, the winds picked up and the swell size increased, which presented more of a physical challenge than a technical one, but regardless we were grateful when we left the open water for the sheltered inlet of Long Island. Our timing was perfect because shortly after we left the open water, the weather turned and the sea roiled in a frothy chop, yet in the safety of the protected channel we paddled hard on calm water, in the fading light.

The wind continued to pick up intensity after we got off the water, turning those large swells into a series of dangerous and powerful breakers, capable of easily capsizing kayaks paddled by tired racers. We later learned that the paddle was closed by race officials due to the severity of the storm and that teams were scattered along most of the route, either stopped at checkpoints or taking shelter along the shorelines of some of the many islands in an attempt to avoid Nature's Fury. One thing these races are good at is reminding me that we have no control over Mother Nature, so if she's in a rotten mood, your best bet is to stay inside and wait her out. This storm split the field, giving us some breathing room in case we required it later in the race. Lady Luck was on our side this time.

Years of racing have let me in on a little secret that I like to call the "out of sight, out of mind" advantage. If you can build a significant lead of several hours—even if it grows or shrinks by ten to twenty minutes—it will serve as a solid buffer that is often impossible for trailing teams or athletes to overcome, and that's critical in adventure racing, ultrarunning, and other long-distance endurance events. If you can work hard enough to open a gap that takes you out of sight, your competitors typically fall into a more complacent state where they settle into a "defend and protect the current position" mentality instead of a "must chase down the leader wherever the heck they are" mentality. Chasing is hard work, especially when you can't see your prey and thus don't quite know how to gauge your effort. It leaves you with a choice: Do I redline it at full gas to close the gap, which may be very large, and risk blowing up and losing my position, or do I instead race conservatively and hope to capitalize on an error by the leader? Because of this, it's infuriatingly hard to close these time gaps. I've seen it time and time again from both sides.

Accordingly, having a small lead where you never vanish from sight is more of a disadvantage than an advantage. Basically, if a competitor can keep you in view, you act as their carrot—dangling there tantalizingly and seemingly within reach. This gives the chasers hope, and it can spur them to race faster than they otherwise would, as they can calculate the effort required to catch you and may realize that they still have the stamina to push hard enough to do it. In adventure racing, it gives them the added benefit of seeing your navigational decisions and profiting from them.

During a thirty-six-hour adventure race in Digby, New Brunswick, I learned firsthand the value of being the hunter instead of the hunted. As the hunter, you have the luxury of knowing how to gauge your efforts, especially when you know where your prey is, as we did in this case. Taking advantage of this situation and finding the perfect blend of patience and good navigation were the key to winning my first adventure race. Six hours into the race, we were on our mountain bikes and had been patiently following a team for over thirty minutes, biding our time until the conditions were right to make our move. Reaching an intersection, we faced a critical navigational decision: surge ahead now or later. I knew our team still had some matches left to burn and that, if we waited a little longer, we'd have an opportunity to use our fitness to pass the lead team and hold them off, so we rode fast enough to keep them in sight but slow enough not to give our position away just yet.

The topographic maps we receive in adventure races are notoriously old and often do not reflect the current geographic conditions. Roads shown on old maps are often badly overgrown, and new roads cut after the printing of the map are conspicuously absent, which leave us guessing a lot of the time. This intersection was one of those instances. Spirit, one of Canada's best teams and the current leader, had stopped and were discussing its options. We said our hellos as we rode up and chatted briefly. Jayme, who had been a flawless navigator the entire race, was sure that we were supposed to head straight through the intersection. Now, in adventure racing, terrible mistakes can be made by following other teams blindly. Not only is this frowned on, it also means that you're trusting them with your important decisions, something most navigators will tell you is a cardinal sin. Navigation decisions should only be made based on the navigator's understanding of where your team is. If teams go with the flow, not only are they prone to being led off course, but often it's very hard to relocate themselves on the map once they realize the error.

We sat at the intersection, waiting. We knew we wanted to continue in the direction of travel that had brought us there, but I wanted to see which way team Spirit was going to go. As it turned out, they had other ideas and headed to the left. We waited for them to commit to their choice and then hit the gas, dropping the hammer in a big way so that by the time they realized their error, we'd be well ahead—way out of sight. Jayme was right, the tactic paid off, and we went on to secure our first adventure racing win in a record time—and over an hour ahead of Spirit, the second-place team. Call it good luck or good strategy, knowing what the lead dogs are doing can benefit you in many ways.

A similar scenario recently played out in season two of *Boundless*, when Turbo and I found ourselves competing

Can You Pick Out the Leader of the Pack?

It can be dangerous business to judge a book by its cover. When I was twenty-three, I jumped into a local 5K on a whim in order to start improving my running. Looking around the start line, I saw the usual spread of fit-looking speedsters to first timers, but a young girl in a two-piece outfit caught my eye. Significantly shorter than the runners nearby, she stood out. I thought, *That's cute. A little girl wanting to look like a real runner, just like Mom and Dad.* When the gun started, this girl set out at a sub-twenty-minute pace. I ran behind, thinking to myself, *Jeez, her parents are pushing her a bit hard so early in this race. They should probably dial it back so they don't blow her up.* At the halfway point, she was several hundred yards ahead of me. Suffice to say I was dumbfounded and definitely humbled, although I still expected to pass her after her inevitable explosion. That explosion never happened and she finished in a blistering time of 19:23, over two minutes faster than me! She was eleven years old and one of the fastest athletes on the day. I hear stories like this all the time: some athletes are overly confident without having the training to back it up, while others are intimidated by fit-looking competitors, shaved legs, and shiny new gear. When we line up, it's important to take stock of your competition, but looks can be deceiving. It's more crucial to remember what you've done to get there and to avoid playing the race out in your head before even taking the first step. Run your own race and everything will fall into place.

in the three-day, 115-mile Amazing Amazon Raft Race in Peru. The race required teams of four to paddle *home-made* balsa rafts—yes, we only had an afternoon to literally build these—down the Amazon River over three stages. We paired with the husband-and-wife team of Justin and Jesse White, who were keen adventurers but not quite at our level of fitness. Over the first two days, we battled for second place against a team of American paddlers. We took day one, and they beat us on day two, so the third and final stage was for all the marbles and prize money. The final stage was a long and grueling paddle on the Amazon River near Iquitos, Peru (noteworthy for being the largest city in the world with no road access), where the water was the color of chocolate milk and flowed at little more than a walking pace.

We started the day strong, pulling ahead of the Americans and opening up a sizable lead, but at some point our fatigue caught up to us, we unknowingly let off the gas, and the Americans caught and passed us. I could see that we had hit a low but encouraged the team on. Because the river was so slow, I knew that it required a massive effort to get the boats moving fast and that any big moves would result in an inevitable slowdown after-ward. With this in mind, I had the team paddle just fast enough to keep the Americans in sight and in striking dis-tance, approximately four hundred meters downstream.

I knew that if we were going to pass them and hold them off, we'd need to do two things well: time it perfectly and paddle with such speed and confidence that we'd bluff our way back on the podium. Again, easier said than done. We paddled in a steady rhythm, cutting through the sediment-rich waters of the Amazon at a comfortable pace that we could sustain for hours. I studied the Americans as we inched ever closer to the finish line, patiently waiting for their pace to slow. As we approached the final few kilometers of the race, I noticed that we had gained ground on the other boat and I knew that our time to pounce was at hand. With mounting excitement, we hit the gas, building to a full head of steam as we passed the American boat and left it helpless in our wake. We had surprised them and continued to paddle at top speed for another ten minutes, opening a gap of several hundred meters in the process. We held that lead as we turned off of the main channel into a tributary that required two kilometers of exhausting upstream paddling to reach the finish line. Once inside this tributary we took a break to recover. Now, back in second place and on the podium, we found another gear to hold off the charging Americans until the finish line. I always look back on this race as one where racing at the front of the pack created good luck by invigorating the team and giving them a sense of purpose, which helped us all find hidden strength to push hard for the podium. Each day we paddled with a sense of purpose and a seemingly endless supply of courage, heart, and stamina when we needed it.

In both the Digby race and on the Amazon, being patient when it mattered allowed us to conserve energy, remain relaxed, and stay focused on making good decisions without any pressure. After we hit the gas, we opened up enough of a lead that we didn't have to worry about other teams either profiting from our decisions in Nova Scotia or passing us in the final kilometers in Peru.

The same has been true in my businesses, Adventure Science and Stoked Oats. Both have been leaders in their respective areas. Adventure Science was the first citizen science organization to pair athletes and scientists, and Stoked Oats was one of Canada's early adopters of gluten-free oatmeal. Whether you are leading the pack or silently following in wait for your opportunity to move to the front, I've found that, more often than not, it pays to be first or close enough to the front to see what the leaders are doing and be able to respond quickly.

8.

A Tired Body (Almost) Always Follows a Determined Mind

When I was younger, I used to look at physical or mental challenges and think, *I can do that* or *I can't do that*—and I was right. The mind plays a critical role in determining just how far we can go and how long we can push even when we are exhausted. Nowhere, though, is the power and limits of mind over matter more obvious that in adventure races and ultramarathons, where we race on little to no sleep for a day or more.

My first Eco-Challenge served up some of the worst sleep monsters that I've ever had to contend with. *Sleep monsters* refers to the state in which adventure racers have to use all of their mental might to stave off sleep and continue competing. We were nearly halfway through the race and had reached a transition area that marked the start of a long mountain bike leg. We ate quickly and then began the unenviable task of building our bikes, which were transported in hard-shell cases during the event. We dragged our bike boxes into a barn located next to the transition area to build our bikes and get out of the light rain that was falling. I examined my bike parts after pulling them from the case and noticed that the chain was twisted into a kinked mess. I struggled with it, trying to figure out this puzzle I held in my now grease-covered hands, made clumsy from a lack of sleep. At this point, we had only slept for around four hours, definitely not long enough to be an effective problem solver in this situation. My cognitive skills were starting to fade by then, three days in.

Research has shown a progressive breakdown in humans' motor skills, as well as their ability to concentrate, think clearly, or even to stay motivated, after prolonged periods of sleeplessness. I was unknowingly experiencing textbook symptoms of sleep deprivation. My solution to the twist in my chain was not to ask for help but to disassemble part of the bike in order to access the chain and untwist it. Lucky for me, that plan worked. Unfortunately, I dropped one of the bolts in the straw on the barn floor during the process. I began to search, but with each passing moment that I couldn't find it, my sense of panic grew. Without this bolt, I would be unable to use the gears on my bike—not the ideal situation considering the massive mountain ride ahead of us. "Jeff," I called out, "I need your help." Jeff was building his bike next to mine and immediately joined me in my "needle in a haystack" search. We got lucky and dodged a major bullet when Jeff triumphantly pulled the bolt out of the straw in a race-saving discovery.

With that minor catastrophe avoided, we headed out into the cool night air for a tedious and lengthy mountain bike ride/hike-a-bike. We hadn't been riding very long before I ran up against another sleep deprivation–induced hurdle. I was waging war against the sleep monsters as we rode the first few kilometers of the wide mountain roads. The grade was flat, only punctuated by the odd small hill. The road surface was a mix of smooth gravel and up-to-fist-sized rocks. In my deliriously tired state, I found myself constantly hitting these larger rocks and coming to a dead stop, or falling off my bike. I had literally lost the ability to move my bike forward over this terrain. If I didn't get some sleep soon, there was no way that I'd be able to function as we rode into the bigger, steeper, and more technical terrain that awaited us. Even though the rest of the team was able to push on, we had to stop. I was quoted in advance of this race by my university newspaper as saying, "We'll sleep if the whole team can lie down and go right to sleep. Otherwise, there's no point in one person sleeping." Sometimes the best intentions go out the window when you're faced with a real-life crisis. My lack of sleep had left me completely and utterly impaired. Little did we know that, while I was hitting the wall at the start of the mountain bike leg, over a hundred kilometers ahead of us, Kiwi Nathan Fa'avae, one of the stars of the sport, had also become completely incapacitated by lack of sleep and had forced his team to rest, thus allowing the dominant American team Salomon/Eco-Internet to do what they had been unable to do since the start of the race, and pass them, holding on for the win.

The brief nap restored my faculties enough for us to continue riding through the night and into the next day. By the time we reached the end of the bike section, we were just outside of the top ten, and two paddles and a mountain trek from the finish—although getting there would take another thirty-six hours. After completing a major hike around an island to which we had paddled our rafts, we readied ourselves for our final paddle through a series of braided rivers and the lake.

We paddled as hard as we could, in part to preserve our tenth-place position but also just to get this miserable bastard over and done with. "I'll be honest—when you race, sometimes you just hate it, and I certainly did at that point. When you finish, you're happy and a couple days later you think to yourself, 'I just covered however many kilometers, faced these adversities, and passed the test that was presented to me,'" I said later in an interview. Despite the looming finish line, I was on the ropes during the final paddle, dealing with intense hallucinations and barely able to keep my head up. I lost track of the passing kilometers as I drifted in and out of sleep en route to the finish line. Exhaustion had finally caught up with me and I employed my patented sleep-paddling technique, which is very similar to my sleep-walking and sleep-riding techniques. I'd sleep until my team would wake me, at which point I'd snap to attention, paddle hard for a while, and then drift away with a prolonged "blink." It didn't matter, though; we were now within view of the finish line and crossing it was inevitable.

I was elated afterward but more tired than I have ever been in my life. My good friend Chris Frantz, who while traveling New Zealand on a gap year along with Pete had come to cheer us to the finish of the race, gave me some coins for the campground shower to wash five days, eighteen hours, and forty-nine minutes of sweat and filth away. It was glorious. I stood there in that cramped and dirty campground shower stall, savoring every minute of that brief shower experience. From there, I went to the tent Chris had set up for me and I was probably snoring before my head even hit the pillow.

I slept on the bus ride back to Queenstown, woke briefly to unload gear and check into my room (which I shared with Jeff), and promptly fell back to sleep. I slept, dead to the world for over twenty hours in that darkened bedroom. Jeff later told me that people were coming in to check on me and take my pulse, as everyone else seemed to be fine with only eight to ten hours of sleep. I slept for nearly a day straight. That record still stands for me and I jokingly tell friends who lament about difficulty sleeping to go race the Eco-Challenge—it would put the worst insomniac to sleep.

I came out of this experience thinking that if I was able to push myself that hard for nearly six days of racing on less than two hours of sleep per day, then there was no excuse in my regular life for not getting things done. While I'm not advocating living a life without sleep, the body is an incredible machine capable of following orders. If the brain asks, the body responds.

When you're riding through hilly terrain in the dark and on no sleep, the normal challenge of a climb or descent reaches a new level. I remember being proud of how I could sleep-ride. I'd mastered the technique of sleep walking earlier in my adventure racing life. When I was exhausted but had to keep moving, I'd close my eyes and stumble along, mildly aware of what I was walking on. This technique only worked on wide, smooth gravel roads, where the risk of walking off the road or into a ditch was minimal. This technique worked especially well when someone was towing you, which is a common practice in adventure racing, as a bit of pull from a bungee cord tied to your waist belt or chest strap gives you enough energy to keep up with your teammates when they are moving faster than you. I remember my teammate Sarah's battles with her sleep monsters during the Beast of the East in 2001, most of which resulted in babbling, hallucinations, and a drunken stagger down the road. Dangerous as it was, we were young and wanted to reach the podium so badly that sleep walking, or even sleep riding, was considered acceptable and preferable to stopping and sleeping. As I matured as an adventure racer, I grew to see the value in sleeping, as even a bit of rest can recharge athletes, allowing them to race faster, shake the mental fog, and make better decisions. I now plan sleep into my race strategy for multiday races. For me, the time to sleep is now usually when the entire team is starting to slow substantially, when one team member is totally wiped, or when an opportunity presents itself due to weather that slows or stops progress. The ideal situation is for everyone to sleep when the team stops, although this isn't always possible.

In these races you reach a level of fatigue where you can literally sleep anywhere or doing anything. Prior to the Beast of the East race, I had experienced this once during a five-day expedition race in 1999 with some friends from Michigan, Ryan Kennedy, Ryan Benson, and Lauren Schelenberger, whom we called Little Thunder.

The Two-Week Rule

During *Boundless*, whenever I tease Turbo for mentioning his age and performance in the same breath, he replies, "Just wait until you're fifty, dude," implying that his victories are all the more impressive because he's got a few more aches and pains to deal with than I do. We are living longer and better than we ever have in the history of our species, which has allowed us to compete in sport well into our golden years. As a result, many of us suffer wear-and-tear athletic injuries. In my twenties and early thirties, I gave myself a two-week rule for this type of injury. If something started to hurt during training or racing, I'd give it two weeks to improve, while taking time off and engaging in rehabilitative strength training. If it hadn't started to improve by the end of two weeks, then I'd go see a doctor but not before. As athletes, we all tend to freak out when we get injured, but I've learned that the body—when rested, fueled, and destressed properly—will heal on its own and at its own pace, without medical intervention. Now that I'm in my forties, I give myself closer to three weeks. As you gain greater bodily awareness and become more attune to your "baseline," you'll be able to recognize the onset of certain types of overuse injuries in the early stages and stop them before they manifest into something more severe. Recognizing injuries early and managing my recovery, I've been able to race three grueling seasons of *Boundless* thanks to my two-week rule.

After racing for five days through the wilderness of northern Ontario, we had reached the beginning of a paddle that marked the final leg of the race. We had about thirty kilometers of sea kayaking through the tempestuous north channel of Georgian Bay between us and the finish line. We were all delirious with fatigue when we pushed off shore in our boats early that final morning. The water was calm, and the sun was just appearing above the horizon— ideal conditions to paddle through and to savor our pending accomplishment, which was coincidentally my first expedition length race (of five days or more). Ryan Kennedy sat in the front of my boat and, unfortunately, in his exhausted state, navigated us in the wrong direction, costing us about two hours. I remember our discussion once he realized his mistake. We were both so tired and so confused that we thought the compass might have been affected by magnetized iron minerals in the rocky islands and that we couldn't trust it. It took far too long for our foggy brains to understand the simple fact that we had gone west when we should have gone east.

Once we recognized our error and got back on track, we started getting into rougher water as a storm slowly rolled in. We paddled feverishly as the storm intensified and the waves grew, their foamy crests slapping against the sides of our kayak with an unnerving regularity. We narrowly stayed ahead of the worst of the storm, hitting remote island checkpoints before the race directors closed them down due to the dangerous conditions. We later learned that we had moved through two checkpoints like this, and they had closed within thirty minutes of us leaving them. As the tempest grew, the waves began to break over the boat. It was all I could do to keep the boat on the correct bearing, as the mountain of water obscured the landmasses we were using to navigate. Our nylon spray skirts were loose-fitting and filled with water like a bathroom sink. I would paddle several hard strokes and then take one hand off the paddle to bail like crazy with that free hand, as the water, sloshing in the drowned spray skirt, was upsetting the buoyancy of the kayak. The water got higher until we found ourselves in a wave trough, no longer able to see Benson and Little Thunder in their boat. Unbeknownst to me, the waves that relentlessly battered us that afternoon reached twelve feet in height. It was a very bad day to be on the water.

At this point, we knew that we were in some serious danger. The coast guard would not be able to get boats out in this storm; if one of us capsized, we'd be risking hypothermia for sure and possibly drowning. I was scared but full of adrenaline and completely focused on keeping the boat upright. I wish I could have said the same for Ryan, who was slumped forward, paddle resting on the deck of the kayak, fast asleep. We were literally in the

worst situation we could imagine, our lives were in danger, and he was so tired that he couldn't stay awake. I
was floored. "Ryan," I shouted. "Wake up, man! You need
to paddle." He would snap to life, paddle a few strokes,
and then, as fatigue overtook his will to live, I'd watch
his paddling trail off. First, the blade would miss the
water for a stroke, then he'd be paddling in the air, and
finally, the paddling would stop altogether. Then we'd
repeat the process.

We made the decision to beach the boats on a small,
rocky island that we had spotted in the distance through
the storm. We had been on the water for over eight hours
at that point. Although we were within fifteen kilometers
of the finish, we decided that, after five days of racing, it
was time to play it safe rather than let the storm play rou-
lette with our lives any longer. There are always other
podiums to chase and races to enter. I cut the foot rudder
to take us toward the island, surfing the steep, breaking
face of the waves and then tacking at the bottom to ensure
we hit the island. After we paddled like this for fifteen
exhausting minutes, a final, large wave picked us up and
dumped us on the rocky island with such force I thought
the hull would surely crack. We sprang from the boat on
shaking legs, numb from the hours in the boat, and
dragged the kayak above the breaking waves. I had
never seen the effects of fatigue like that before—and it

was scary. I realized that day that an overly tired racer is in a precarious position. Fatigue in an adventure race can catch you off guard, rendering you useless even in the most demanding of situations. I'm still amazed at how few serious injuries and fatalities happen in this sport, considering the exposure to risk that can occur. This was my first experience with extreme fatigue while racing, but it certainly wasn't my last.

Although I really dislike acknowledging boundaries, there are limits to endurance and human performance that all athletes need to respect. To ignore these limits or imagine that you are immune to them is simply arrogant and foolhardy. I have pushed myself to the brink of exhaustion numerous times but have never had a close call that put me in the hospital, although I have witnessed it happen to others. We were racing a 250 km staged running race in Cambodia in season one of *Boundless*. I was having a terrible race—completely out of gas and struggling both physically and mentally. It was the third day and we had a 75 km jungle run to complete, mostly on dirt roads where there was little relief from the sun. The air was extremely hot and very humid. I managed to run the first ten kilometers but then simply gave up and started walking, determined to finish the stage but no longer interested in running another step that day. After several hours of walking, the two females battling for the lead came by, less than five minutes apart. My friend Sophie, whom I had met months earlier while racing in Iceland, was sitting in second place overall in the women's field and had a chance to take the lead if she won the day. We walked and talked for a while and then she headed off running again, determined to win the stage, which she did. When I crossed the finish line several hours later, I saw Sophie lying on a stone block, silent, motionless, and with a glazed look on her face. I gave out some high fives, said a quick hello to Sophie, and then headed toward my tent to connect with Turbo and see how his day had gone. (He had a great stage, finishing second on the day and catapulting onto the overall podium.) In winning, Sophie had pushed herself to the brink and beyond. Nobody knew it at the time, but through the effort of the day, she had depleted her electrolytes (minerals such as calcium, potassium, and sodium that are carried in our bloodstream and allow the body to maintain an electrical charge at the cellular level, necessary for the functioning of muscles and nerves) and was now suffering from hyponatremia, a potentially fatal condition. Her health worsened through the evening, and despite receiving intravenous fluids, her body went into shock and seizure the following afternoon. Up until that point she had wanted to continue racing, but thankfully the race director was able to talk her out of it. She was airlifted to the hospital in Siem Reap. Fluid on the brain prevented the doctors from seeing her brain activity, so she was then relocated to Bangkok, and doctors were finally able to stabilize her. Fortunately, she pulled through and is still running and doing great as a new mom, wife, and executive. Hers was definitely a happy ending to a very scary and potentially fatal situation. Sophie's story reminds me that while it's good to go hard in life and sport, we have to know ourselves and when to throw in the towel. Humans are resilient creatures, but we are not invincible. I have a file folder of X-rays to attest to this fact.

9.

Invest in the Fun Bank

Races can involve a lot of hard, tedious sections so it's important to have a ready supply of distractions to prevent you from dwelling on them. That's where the *fun bank* comes in, an imaginary bank where you make deposits every time you do something fun in the race. "Wow, that was a great downhill section"— add it to the fun bank. "Man, I can't believe how great that white water was"—put another coin in the fun bank. It's important that the fun bank is well stocked, because there will be times in every race when you have to make withdrawals from the bank, especially during those sections that are just miserable and feel like work. All work and no play makes Jack a dull boy. If racing, training, and our jobs are only about the work, they quickly lose their luster, so I make sure to invest in the fun bank when I'm undertaking long and difficult projects.

As we approached the end of our first season of *Boundless*, both Turbo and I were pretty shattered. Not only had we taken on a series of massively challenging races, we had done it in around four months—a tall order for any endurance athlete. Turbo was homesick, and I was battling injury and a fatigue that had hit me hard in Cambodia, as I delivered a very up-and-down performance during those seven days. We had one race left to do: a half Ironman in Phuket, Thailand. I had always wanted to visit Thailand, and Phuket in particular, while Turbo was drawn to the islands off the coast that boasted some world-class rock climbing. We worked with Steven and Josh to integrate a trip to the islands into the episode. We viewed this as a fun recovery—something to take our minds off of the upcoming race, which was only seven days after the Cambodia stage race. With no real time to fully rest our weary bodies, we figured that we should at least work on letting our minds recover.

We traveled by longtail boat to Krabi and hired a guide to take us out to some small islands that had deepwater free solo climbing routes, which is a fancy way of saying unbolted rock climbing routes without any ropes. You climb over the ocean and, if you fall, you land in the water. I found it absolutely exhilarating to have that freedom and feel like every move truly matters because there is no safety rope to catch you. Despite the fatigue that plagued me, I thrived and climbed long and challenging routes without fear. I was having fun and that gave me more than enough energy to thrive. By the time we had finished that day of climbing, we were both on top of the world and mentally ready to take on our final challenge. In a way, taking time out to do something fun fueled my inner fire and rejuvenated me for that last episode.

The fun bank can also serve as a distraction to help keep your mind off of a looming challenge or deadline. The Amazing Amazon Raft Race was a surprisingly difficult race for us. The heat was incredible, the sun baked us, and the water moved sluggishly. We spent between five and eight hours daily paddling our raft with hands that were blistered from using handmade balsa paddles. Turbo and I were physically and mentally wiped before even stepping onto the raft for day one, having recently returned from two massive back-to-back races in Europe (Ramsay's Round and SUP 11 City Tour). We needed something to give us a boost, as our boats didn't have exceptional hydrodynamics and the water moved extremely slowly. These factors, coupled with the heat, made this race one of the most difficult that I have competed in to date. Each night, the race directors would turn the staging area just beyond the competitors' tents into a makeshift disco in order to give us energy. They served beer on the river barge and encouraged everyone to get out of their tents and dance as they blasted their Latino dance songs on full volume. Initially, it was infuriating because all

Find Your Zen

My best ideas have always come to me when I step away from the desk and go outside for a run, ride, paddle, or ski. Leaving my modern distractions behind for an hour or more each day has given me time to reflect on my life, businesses, and athletics. When I'm under the gun with deadlines or feeling pressure to be creative, that is when I need my exercise break the most, as I return with a clear mind, focused thoughts, and greater energy. The first time I really noticed this benefit was during the final stages of writing my PhD dissertation on tsunamis. Sitting at my desk, I would struggle to rationalize data sets or to think through scenarios related to the evidence I had collected. During my daily training ride on my road bike, though, my body and mind would relax, and the pressure to produce or resolve issues would vanish. Once that happened, I was free to let my mind wander and even daydream, which was usually a catalyst for new ideas or solutions to problems I was having. These rides represented quiet, uninterrupted time for thought and creativity as much as for training my aerobic capacity. Once I started my working life as a geologist, the value of physical activity was reinforced at the corporate gym I frequented daily, as I would regularly see senior management making time to exercise, even if it was just for fifteen to thirty minutes on a busy day.

we wanted to do was sleep and prepare for the next day, but this soon became something comical that we looked forward to. Would they add lasers to the party tonight? Would there be another conga line? Although we didn't participate in the dance party, it did become something that made us laugh, lightened the mood, and took our minds off of racing for a while each night.

My team also made good use of the fun bank whenever we could at the 2001 Eco-Challenge. En route to the first paddle of the race, a whitewater rafting leg that would last most of the daylight hours on that second day, we hit our first rope section—a zipline that carried us over a raging mountain river. The organizers felt there was too big of a risk for the athletes to face in crossing it, so they strung the lines. While it felt slightly contrived, it was still a break in the trek and a contribution to the fun bank. Riding a zipline is always great because in these races it's time off your feet, there is a rush that comes with the speed of flying along over land or water, and it's an easy way to get an adrenaline rush. In this case, we crossed a beautiful river early in the morning, so the mist was rising off of the quiet water in the distance, the sun was starting to illuminate the mountain peaks, and we could hear the rushing sound of the water. These sights and sounds reminded me to take it all in, let go of the race, and just enjoy this effortless experience. Unbeknownst to us, we finished our zipline mere kilometers away from the first of the sections where we'd really need to draw on those fun memories.

Paddling sections are usually the least mentally stimulating of a race. Hours of paddling less-than-ideal vessels in a variety of water conditions usually works to put the mind into hibernation. This race was touted as having epic white water, so we were all looking forward to the first paddle, which started in a braided river but then spilled into Lake Pukaki, a large north–south trending lake about twenty kilometers long.

The fun bank withdrawals started as soon as we reached the rafting section and learned that we had to portage our raft nearly five hundred meters to the edge of the river. Without a trail to follow, we were forced to carry the heavy raft over boulders and cobbles, tripping and falling as we went. While it wasn't long, it was an exercise in perseverance and positive thinking. It was easy to get annoyed, frustrated, and bitter because we felt that the race directors were just creating additional drama for the television broadcast rather than challenges necessary for the race.

Paddling a braided river system is a little like gambling, as numerous chutes and channels appear and you have to continually make quick decisions about whether to take them or not. The goal is to always stay in the channel that has the greatest flow. This keeps you moving fast but also helps ensure that you don't hit a dead-end channel, which is common in this type of river system. Our luck was good that morning, and we didn't have to drag our raft through many dead ends, so we were able to keep pace with the teams around us.

Eventually, the river spat us into Lake Pukaki, and we took a major withdrawal from the fun bank. Inflatable rafts are great to paddle in white water because of their stability and durability. On open water, and without a current, though, they are a nightmare. They are clunky, have tremendous drag, and are not easy to steer. In a word, they are pigs. This was not the fun paddling that had been advertised. We slowly paddled into the wind on the lake, inching along at a snail's pace. Eventually, due to a strong headwind, which made paddling even more difficult, we opted to hike the raft along the shoreline using a technique called lining. To do this, we attach two ropes to the boat—one at the bow, the other at the stern—and two members of the team hold the ropes and walk along the shore, allowing the raft to float just far enough offshore so as to not bounce off the shoreline rocks but close enough to keep the raft from the wind.

This was actually a big improvement and something of a relief initially; however, walking a long distance in a wetsuit can lead to chafing issues. For me, it was my upper thighs and groin that were starting to chafe. In an effort to prevent further injury, and lacking any anti-chafing cream, I grabbed the lidocaine (a topical anesthetic cream for cuts and burns) and jogged ahead of the team in order to apply it to my hot spots. What happened next is still talked about when the team gets together and reminisces about the race. Never having used the cream before, I didn't know much about it, other than the fact that it claimed on the tube to offer burn relief. Well, as I discovered after I dropped my unzipped wetsuit and shorts and applied the cream, what it actually did was make my chafed spots feel like they were suddenly on fire. When the team rounded the bend in the lake, they had a visual that they'd have just as soon forgot. Naked, with my wetsuit and shorts around my ankles and my crotch on fire from the ointment, I was running and jumping around and yelling at my team, "Don't use the lidocaine on open wounds—it burns, it burns!" That day I learned that trying new products on race day is a rookie mistake. The team got more than an eyeful but also a good laugh—money back into the fun bank (or, in this case, the "thanks for making us laugh" bank).

Home Is Where
the Trail Runners Are

I've always tried to live in beautiful places with easy access to trails and nature. I moved to Canmore, Alberta, in 2012 to train and play in the mountains, one of the best decisions I've ever made. Not only am I surrounded by inspiring wilderness, but the small-town setting suits my nature extremely well. Add to that a close-knit group of friends with whom I share many adventures, and I feel right at home. Working from home, it is important to me to have inspiration and nature at my fingertips. A glance out the window at Mount Lady Macdonald's snowcapped peak or an hour-long trail run with Phil Villeneuve are commonplace occurrences that kept me at my best. Living a life on the road while filming *Boundless* or traveling for Adventure Science projects has been stressful, but that stress has always melted away when I see the mountains on the drive home from the airport, because I know that the tranquility of the small mountain town is only an hour away. Maintaining our physical and mental health requires more than exercise, but I've found that much of it comes from enjoying where you live and having the freedom to roam. Houses and apartments can be bought or sold, so don't let the trappings of possessions tie you down. By living in a place you want to draw inspiration from, you'll be able to lead a happier and more fulfilling life.

10.

Make Deals with Yourself

I've often thought that we are the biggest barrier to our own success. Humans are very good at rationalizing why we should avoid, or stop doing, difficult tasks. This unfortunate phenomenon is common in endurance sports, but, if you are aware of it, there are some simple little hacks that you can use to motivate yourself or others to get moving or push harder. I like to call it *activation energy*—a term I stole from high school chemistry class. Officially, activation energy is the minimum amount of energy required to initiate a chemical reaction. Once that reaction is rolling along, it doesn't take much energy to sustain it, so the biggest challenge is providing the energy required to get it started. I use it as a metaphor to help me do things that I've been reluctant to do. This could be getting out the door to train, pushing harder into the red zone on an interval run, or simply doing my monthly finances. In order to get the activation energy I need to complete the project, I often make deals with myself or use self-talk to encourage and psych myself up to the point where I want to take on the challenge. This technique has served me in all my races, with one of the most classic examples coming from my first Eco-Challenge race in 2001.

When I'm in race-mode, my motivation comes from the little proverbial carrots—food, drink, warmth, sleep, the cheering of the crowd, a looming finish line, etc. It was day four and the sun was hot. We were nearing the end of an incredibly long and grueling mountain bike stage and were pushing hard on a blacktop road. We started talking about ice cream for some reason. Ice cream is one of those things that can make anyone happy, especially if you've been hiking, paddling, and biking through the New Zealand backcountry for the previous four days and eating a lot of gels and bars. We agreed that we would stop if we saw a place for ice cream, although the scarcity of buildings along our route made this a wishful proposition. Eventually, we rode past the Wanaka Airport and noticed that there was a cafeteria, which undoubtedly sold ice cream, in the adjacent National Transport and Toy Museum (I still have no idea how transportation and toys combine to make this very unique museum). We pulled our bikes against the windows in order to keep an eye on them while inside, and then we entered the museum in search of that icy goodness. Although we were the only racers in the building, we were not the only patrons in the cafeteria, and we must have created quite the spectacle. My recollection is of the four of us sitting around a circular table, drifting in and out of consciousness, trying to eat our ice cream before it melted on us and the floor. It was comical. After spending far too much time slumped at our table, we eventually dragged our weary bodies outside to resume our ride toward the looming finish line.

However, the deals we make aren't always palpable; sometimes we chase a feeling or emotion. While racing in Egypt during season one of *Boundless*, I found myself making both kinds of deals with myself as I came up against a new obstacle: extreme heat. I'm often asked which races were the toughest for me and, from a physical-suffering perspective, it was the 250 km 4 Deserts Sahara Race in Egypt. I had never experienced, let alone run in, such hot conditions and had to quickly adapt both physically and mentally to cope with the drama that was going on inside of me on a daily basis.

Day one was a 37 km warm-up that served as an emphatic "Hi, I'm the Sahara Desert and if you want to finish this thing, you're going to have to get through me!" I went hard off the line, quickly realizing that I would able to run faster on firmer sand if I stayed out front, instead of following behind runners who churned it up. I started to fade around ten kilometers into the leg and by the fifteenth kilometer four runners, including Turbo, had passed me. I hit a low and walked for a while to regain my stamina. One month after getting injured in Kenya, I was running with trekking poles to take some of the weight off my knee and, in the sand, I felt like they gave me the added benefit of four-wheel drive. Eventually, I resumed running and managed to run down two of the athletes who had passed me earlier, finishing third on the day. Turbo had a great run and put about fifteen minutes into me while a Spaniard named Vicente Juan Garcia had dominated everyone, winning by fifteen minutes and setting a trend that would continue the rest of the week.

Although I had struggled that day, I was overjoyed that I was able to run without any knee issues. Sure, I had wilted in the heat, but at the same time I learned that the desert doesn't care if you make it or not—your success is based on smart racing. I knew that I'd have to race strategically if I were to have a shot at surviving this race. The first part of being strategic is recovering well. We were allocated four liters of water per person per day for drinking, plus the water provided at each aid station and whatever we used for our dehydrated meals. Reaching the finish line, we would savor the shade, sitting for fifteen to thirty minutes, drinking water, and letting our bodies cool down. For me, making it to the finish line to bask in the luxurious shade was the big carrot each day. The deal I had made with myself was to simply do whatever it took to get out of the relentless heat and into the shade of the finishers' tent as fast as I could each day. I accepted that I might need to walk, but the overall goal was always to run as much as possible and then enjoy the shade as long as I wanted. When we had cooled sufficiently, we'd change out of our race gear and eat our lunch—which for me was a dehydrated meal high in calories. I was racing on approximately 2,800 calories per day, and thanks to a past Adventure Science project, I know that I burn around 485 calories per hour when exercising at a 6/10 effort level and in cool-warm conditions. Here, in the desert I estimated that I was burning well over 500 calories per hour— probably somewhere around 600 to 700. With the average stage length hovering around four hours, plus or minus thirty minutes, I'd burn anywhere from 2,400 to 3,200 calories. This would result in a calorie deficit on the day, so once I'd finished eating lunch, I'd find a cool spot to lie down (rarely an easy proposition) and try to sleep as much as possible until the next day—ideally waking only to eat, drink, and do some filming to recap each stage. Conservation of energy and forced recovery was my mantra. As always, I wasn't out there to hit podium necessarily, just to race as hard as I possibly could.

To me, the desert is more than just sand. It's a living tapestry that changes with each puff of the wind, as dunes

One Man's Marathon
Is Another's 5K

After telling some of my *Boundless* war stories at a recent public event, I was approached by a thin but fit-looking young man, who shared how my struggles to persevere had motivated him to break his own boundaries. When I asked him what he was training for, his answer floored me: 5Ks. Even more shocking, however, was his very lofty goal to run a 5K in under fifteen minutes, a goal he was mere seconds away from meeting at the time. He went on to explain that despite the fact that my televised struggles played out over the course of days, instead of minutes and seconds, as his races did, he drew parallels between the two. His fastest 5K to date had come from a race in which he had fallen behind his goal pace early on and his mind had sunk into that dark place where no athlete ever wants to linger . . . and he had contemplated quitting. Then he thought about my Sahara desert race, where I pushed through the heat, gave it my best effort, and made the podium in second place. He committed to finishing the race in that moment and poured it on. The result was his fastest 5K ever. Speaking to him, I realized that the principles of ultra-endurance sports work in all races and even in aspects of our lives and businesses. Despite the fact that a 5K is relatively short, racing at top speed hurts and requires constant mental reinforcement as the body screams for a reprieve. The ability to tell yourself to keep going when it looks like all is lost is the primary characteristic of a winner.

migrate, rock formations erode, and a rising or setting sun draws remarkable color from the dunes. I enjoyed each day, despite the terrible physical toll of running through the sand and heat. I had never run in weather so hot (I recorded 46°C, or 115°F, on my Suunto one day). Prior to Egypt, Kenya had the hottest weather I'd ever run in. Thankfully, the stages started early enough each day that the front runners would usually finish before noon and the peak heat of the day. Mornings in the desert were cool, but by ten o'clock each day the air had heated significantly. Some days we'd have a breeze that kept the heat at bay. Other days, the air was still and there were moments when it felt like I was running inside of an oven.

Over the next few days Vicente Juan ran away from the field. Coming from the hot and dry Alicante region of Spain, this firefighter told me that he found this temperature comfortable. My final run before Egypt had been in the snow. I did not find the heat comfortable; I found it crushing. As the race progressed, the legs became longer, usually pushing past the marathon distance of twenty-six miles. Turbo had a solid lead on me after the first day, which did serve as a carrot to help push me when the running became difficult, even though I was not specifically going after him. I steadily chipped away at Turbo's lead despite the seesaw battle that played out between us daily.

As we moved into the final stage—an 86 km run that would take thirty-six hours for some to complete—the leaderboard solidified. Vicente Juan had a stranglehold on first place. Turbo had dropped out early into the fourth stage due to chafing in his groin, and a Belgian runner named Steven Sleuyter had moved into third place, sitting less than forty minutes behind me. Entering that final stage, I knew that it would test my knee and my resolve in new ways due to the distance and the fact that we would be running through the peak heat of the day.

That day still goes down as my hardest day of running, from a mental perspective. Given that the winner would take at least nine hours, my forty-minute buffer was not an insurmountable lead. The first thirty-seven kilometers went very well, with four of us running in a tight group to the UNESCO world heritage site Wadi Al-Hitan (Whale Valley), an open-air whale fossil museum. My knee felt great, but I was suffering and had been "faking" it the last thirty kilometers. The film crew, driving in air-conditioned SUVs beside us, would roll down the window and ask how I was doing or feeling. In my head, my answer was *I feel like a bag of shit*, but I stayed quiet. I didn't want to let my weakness be known, in case Stevie chose to attack me and force my hand early in the day. To the confusion of Josh and Jordan, I ran mostly in silence, while Turbo cheered me on.

By the 40 km mark, we had dropped our fourth athlete and were pushing up a steep dune two hundred meters high. A gap opened as I failed to match the pace of Vicente Juan and Stevie. I struggled up the dune, sliding backward with each step but eventually making the crest and speeding down the back side to close the gap, which had opened to several hundred meters. Every time Vicente Juan and Stevie would gap me, I'd surge to catch up. Each surge drained me. I didn't know how much longer I could continue to push. It was noon now, and we were nearing peak heat. The breeze that had cooled us through the morning was gone, and we were back to running inside of an oven.

Vicente, a master at pacing, started to pull away from us and by the 45 km mark was lost in the dunes ahead. Almost as if someone had scripted it, it was down to Stevie and me to battle for second. I didn't know it at the time, but he was out of water and opted to hold back. I felt him slow and decided to push to the next aid station, hoping to crack him. While I did beat him to the aid station at the 48 km point, the gap was small and we were soon running together again. It had just passed noon and I was about to experience a level of heat that exceeded that of even the hottest day thus far. I was definitely on the ropes and still had forty kilometers to run.

We left the aid station and started a long, exposed climb on a dusty road leading to a plateau. Stevie passed me early into the climb and started to open a gap. I struggled to catch up to him but was continually dropped until, eventually, I could no longer close the gap. Fifty kilometers into the day, the race was finally on. I was dripping with sweat, walking with my head down, feeling beaten. Rock outcrops loomed in the distance and I considered running the kilometer off course just to stand against the wall and enjoy a sliver of shade. I had never been so hot in my life. It was unescapable. My head throbbed, and I wondered if people's heads ever exploded from the heat. I made a deal with myself that I would walk for half an hour and hopefully recover. I accepted the situation I was in and gave myself a break. For those thirty minutes, I was unconcerned with the competition. I was simply honoring the promise I made to myself.

By the time I'd reached the aid station at sixty kilometers, Stevie had only put five minutes into me despite my walking, but he was out of sight. My forty-minute buffer was beginning to shrink. The aid stations ticked by, and by late afternoon I was running again. The temperature had cooled sufficiently and I was feeling more alive. I still had to talk myself into running, as my legs were sore and weak. I was digging deep but could barely pull anything out. Despite that, I knew I had to keep fighting and figure this thing out one step at a time. I told myself that Stevie was running and that, if I wanted to keep second place, I would have to run, too. Doing this served me well as I adopted a run-walk strategy, continually repeating these deals that I had made with myself during the peak heat in order to find inner strength. I would pick little targets to run toward or set time intervals to either run or walk, and then I'd honor them. I didn't beat myself up over losing ground to Stevie. I accepted that I was suffering; experience told me that if I could just keep moving forward, I would still be in the fight.

Turbo, who had been cheering and fueling me through the aid stations, was keeping me up-to-date on Stevie's lead. By the time I reached the eighth, and final, checkpoint at the 77 km mark, Stevie had eaten away twenty minutes of my lead. Turbo's encouragement helped. It made this brutal solo effort feel more like racing on a team, and not just by myself. It gave me the strength to keep fighting. I knew Stevie would be pushing hard in an effort to do his absolute best. I had to match it.

As I ran the final kilometers toward the finish line, the route started descending into a wide valley. I love running downhills so this motivated me to pick up my pace. I ran and wove my way around small dunes until finally the finish line came into view. My heart swelled with pride and a lump grew in my throat. I felt a surge of energy move through my body and I began to sprint the final few hundred meters. Turbo had come to the end of the finishing chute to high five me, but I was so weak that the simple act almost knocked me over. When I race, I always make a deal with myself that I get to rest when I cross the finish line. Some races I feel strong throughout, while on other days, it is a "mind over matter" situation. My body had given up thirty kilometers earlier and I was just running on guts.

I crossed the finish line, stopped to have my timing card punched with my final time, hugged Turbo, and collapsed. In the episode, I described it as my body shutting down. I fell to the ground and could hear only noise—no voices. I lay there for several seconds before the world came back and I truly realized I was done. I was relieved and happy. My final time for the stage was ten hours, twenty-eight minutes. I had lost twenty-one minutes to Stevie but preserved second place. Both Vicente Juan and Stevie came over to congratulate me. We all hugged, posed for photos, and began to celebrate our achievement. In the end, this race wasn't as much about placing as it was about doing our absolute best against overwhelming odds. I was grateful that my knee had held up for the challenge—another *Boundless* miracle had occurred. I felt for Turbo, who'd had a great race only to be felled by chafing. He would have been a contender for the podium had he continued and may have even reclaimed second, but that is racing. When you toe the start line, you don't always know if you will make the finish. The highs from sharing these experiences with friends—both new and old—are what I end up remembering after these difficult races, not the suffering or wanting to give up. The brutal conditions of this race reminded me that, in life, when the chips are down and your future uncertain, the best way to proceed is to make little deals with yourself, achieve small victories, and relentlessly move forward, regardless of the pace.

11.

There Is No Shame in Surviving

go, in my opinion, is any leader's worst enemy. There are many times in our lives when it's best to retreat from a challenge rather than trying to overcome it at that very moment. I recently found myself in a situation like this, in which my life, and the lives of two friends and teammates, hung in the balance in large part because of our decision to feed our egos. At the end of the day, we learn from mistakes, so there is no shame in retreating when you're up against overwhelming odds and living to fight another day.

In 2014 the Adventure Science team set out to explore one of Madagascar's last frontiers—the Tsingy de Bemaraha, a karst landscape on the western side of the country. Although the south part of the park is known to contain caves, dinosaur tracks, archaeological sites, and lemurs, very little scientific data has been published about the larger northern portion—the Strict Nature Reserve—which can only be explored with the government's permission. The region is a truly unique landscape and biodiversity hot spot that doesn't get the research or tourism attention it should due to brutally difficult terrain and a general absence of infrastructure. The region we were looking to explore was completely off the grid, and we named the project "Madagascar's Limestone Labyrinth" after its suspected physical characteristics. This was Adventure Science's largest project to date and I had assembled a team of twenty athletes, scientists, explorers, communications experts, and support staff. Because it was such a large project, four of us arrived several days ahead of the rest of the team to establish a base camp and to conduct reconnaissance treks. The other three highly experienced adventurers accompanying me were Jim Mandelli, Travis Steffens, and Keith Szlater. Our reconnaissance mission was essential for the success of the project.

The plan was simple: Jim, Travis, and I would head into the tsingy to verify that the survey transects I had plotted in advance were realistic. Adventure Science conducts expeditions to remote, understudied regions, and by pairing endurance athletes with researchers, is able to explore and study the landscape in a manner that conventional approaches cannot. Having conducted a number of high-profile expeditions in the past, the organization was carrying Flag #112 of The Explorers Club on this expedition—an honor shared with many of the last century's greatest explorers.

All mapping, route, and camp selection had been done using fifty-year-old 1:100,000 scale maps and Google Earth images. In other words, we were heading into a 150 by 15 kilometer green blob. There was no additional information available—not from the Park Service and certainly not online. We walked out of camp that morning not knowing if any trails existed in the area where we were heading, if the rivers we'd mapped were still flowing, or how brutal the tsingy rock was in this region.

Uncertainty, however, is something that we accept and plan for when heading into uncharted regions like this, so part of what makes us successful on these expeditions is our ability to adapt. In this case, we would adapt by modifying survey routes based on what we learned from this exploratory hike. We had each packed about eight hours' worth of food and water and carried between us a satellite phone, first aid kit, several GPS units, a cell phone, and several cameras. Upon returning at the end of the day, we would rest and, armed with details about the tsingy, we would greet the rest of the team at the Antsalova airstrip the following morning. With this plan in mind, the three of us posed for a photo and said our goodbyes to our base camp honcho, Keith Szlater, who would be manning the radio all day to maintain communication with us as we explored.

We should have known that we were in for something epic as soon as we crossed the stream that bordered our camp and stepped off the log bridge, immediately impaling ourselves on sharp grasses and getting snagged on thorn-covered vines. At 8:30 a.m., less than an hour into our reconnaissance, it was already 29°C (85°F) and we were drenched in sweat. Perhaps there was a reason that the local Malagasy, as intrepid as they are, avoided the tsingy as a general rule. As the day wore on, we pushed eastward through the heat and dense, "grabby" forest. Two energy-sapping hours and two kilometers later, we hit the tsingy. The tsingy rose out of the forest in front of us like a forgotten and overgrown Angkor temple wall. A highly eroded limestone platform, the tsingy is a geologic formation unique to Madagascar. Translated as the "place where one cannot walk barefoot," this formation is known for its blade-sharp limestone rills, fantastic caves, and unmapped network of interconnected passages. After exploring this wall for several minutes, we discovered a narrow fissure that headed east and directly into it and, without much hesitation, we stepped inside the labyrinth.

Once inside this petrified corn maze, the GPS became useless, the signal pinging wildly trying to connect with satellites. We were back to compass navigation because our maps were of no use. After an hour of walking endless passages, we free-climbed the fifteen meters to the top of the tsingy in order to speed up our progress. While it was clearer on top, we were now fully exposed to the dangerously sharp limestone blades. Maintaining careful footing and balance was imperative. Traversing this terrain was akin to glacier travel in that we were forced to cross numerous crevasses. A fall into any one of these would have been fatal. Each step was calculated and deliberate. Without needing to say a word, the three of us knew how serious this terrain was and that a safe traverse required 100 percent of our focus and attention.

Around one o'clock that afternoon, we made the first of two critical mistakes. After finally crossing what we believed to be the worst of the tsingy, we stopped for a lunch break and to discuss our next steps. We decided to push another hour eastward to verify that we had indeed crossed the most difficult section of the tsingy and gather useful information about that part of the park, helpful for planning the rest of the research expedition. Our enthusiasm and the steadily improving terrain got the best of us and we blew through our sixty-minute contract, hungry for discovery. Still confident and excited, we battled through a maze of limestone outcrops, skirting or scaling endless cliffs. Although we were aware of the danger that surrounded us, we didn't fully appreciate it or acknowledge our vulnerability. In the sweltering heat, we pushed onward.

As the afternoon progressed and darkness drew near, we made our second mistake. We decided that it would be too dangerous to return to camp by backtracking over the worst part of the tsingy in the dark and opted to continue in the hopes of reaching the savannah that bordered the forest on the east. We had seen it from the air and were confident that, once in the savannah, we could trek quickly south for about ten kilometers until we intersected the mapped trail to Antsalova, which we were 90 percent sure existed. We could arrange for a vehicle to meet us there and, if we lucked out, we would arrive just in time to greet the rest of our team when they landed. We radioed to Keith at our base camp and advised him that we would be on the move through the long night. Although he wasn't a fan of the situation, he agreed that it would be too dangerous for us to return in the dark and he established the times for the next updates. We were low on provisions but had encountered large amounts of fresh water on the western side of the tsingy and assumed that water would be equally abundant on the eastern side. We also knew we could handle a night without food, so, with our spirits high, we pushed on into the unknown.

In the darkness, the kilometers ticked slowly by, our route made sinuous by the chaotic geology. We were alarmed to discover that the eastern side of the tsingy was dry. We had been rationing a liter of water throughout the night and had screened and treated some very suspicious-looking water from a tree well and a rock depression that were full of mosquito larvae and decomposing leaves. As we walked, we constantly scanned for water sources, ultimately sipping morning dew from tree leaves and resorting to splitting bamboo shoots to collect the meager amount of water inside. As our slower-than-anticipated pace and depleted rations sunk in and the sun began to rise, a feeling of desperation started to grow inside of me. To make matters worse, we realized that in the best-case scenario, we were still at least a day from Antsalova. We were going to miss the arrival of our team and delay the exploration.

We knew the team, now on the ground and likely wondering why we had not met them on the airstrip, would be starting to get concerned. We had passed out of VHF radio range and had only provided Keith with a terse sat phone update at sunrise, saying that we were still moving toward the grasslands on the eastern edge of the park but our pace had slowed substantially and we were out of water. The stress and pressure of having a team sitting idle at the base camp began to gnaw away at me.

Our Madagascar Adventure Science Team

Due to the remoteness and the physicality of this project, it was important to select a team that could handle the adversity. For this reason, the group was composed of many Adventure Science veterans, including elite ultrarunner and anthropologist Ian MacNairn, and army ranger turned exercise physiologist and obstacle course racer Dr. Tim Puetz. Longtime Adventure Science members Keith and his son-in-law Tyler LeBlanc provided communication and medical support—Tyler bringing a veritable field hospital on his back each day into the tsingy. New additions on the field team included Kensington Tours Explorer-in-Residence Travis, and Canada's best-known storm chaser George Kourounis. Adventure Science publicist Melissa Rae Stewart joined the team to communicate daily findings, and The Explorers Club member Robin Brooks supported the team with communications and camp logistics. In addition to the North American members, our camp bustled with a large Malagasy contingent, including several cooks, 4×4 drivers, gendarmes, park rangers, and local villagers, all hired to support the project.

When most people hear that Adventure Science pairs athletes and scientists to conduct research projects, they often scratch their heads, envisioning a bunch of lithe runners sprinting through forests and up mountains, missing details in the pursuit of speed. This is a common misconception. On expeditions like this, the athletes are first trained by the research lead to become scientific observers before being unleashed into the wild. When the teams are on the move they travel as quickly as the terrain allows, scanning and observing constantly. In addition, they stop at regular intervals to make scientific observations, recording data such as their GPS coordinates and information on the geologic, paleontologic, or anthropologic features. The value the athletes bring is that they have the stamina to conduct daily surveys in demanding terrain and weather conditions, which is rarely possible for researchers in institutional expeditions. Adventure athletes are used to dealing with the physical and mental stress that comes with pushing one's self to the limit, day after day, and instead of caving under the demands, they relish these challenges and thrive. Past expeditions have proven this concept, and as with any Adventure Science project, all findings are documented in a post-expedition report available free of charge at www.adventurescience.com to groups interested in this incredible part of the world.

Despite the financial support provided by our partners, each team member was still spending big bucks to be there. I couldn't shake this feeling that we had put the expedition in jeopardy and—even more gutting—were wasting everyone's time and money as we wandered through tsingy.

I've treated a lot of questionable water over my many years of adventure racing and exploring, but what we ultimately filled our bladders with early on that second morning was the worst by far. Around eight o'clock we stumbled onto a mostly desiccated cattle wallow that held less than a child's swimming pool's worth of scum-covered water in an otherwise dry stream-bed. Instead of mosquito larvae, we siphoned tadpoles and treated the ocher-colored liquid with three chlorine tablets per liter of water (the rule of thumb is one tablet per liter). To prove just how vile this chemical soup was, Jim proceeded to launch into a series of uncontrollable dry heaves after his first swig of our life-saving elixir. We blamed him for causing us to laugh and expend unnecessary calories. The mood was momentarily lightened.

Loaded with water that none of us wanted to drink, we soldiered on into the unrelenting heat, heading toward the savannah and hopefully our salvation. As we crossed illegally burned pastures inside the park boundary, we were optimistic that one of the many cattle tracks would lead us out of the forest and to a village. We marched from pasture to pasture, crossing forested remnants between them, gradually succumbing to the searing heat radiating off this denuded landscape. Our progress slowed to a crawl. We were definitely beyond the point of having fun. This was now becoming desperate work.

Exhausted, down to our last peanuts, and already rationing our precious chemical soup, we trudged to the top of a burned hilltop to get a clear 360-degree view of our surroundings. What we saw was deflating. Aside from the fifty-meter-wide clearing in which we stood, we were surrounded by kilometers of the same thick forest that we'd been battling for the last day and a half. To add insult to injury, we could see Antsalova in the distance—just out of reach on the other side of the forest and the tsingy. This was the tipping point for me as I fully realized the seriousness of our situation. If we continued to press on in our depleted condition, we would be gambling our lives on the prospect of finding more water, which we now knew was a rare commodity on this side of the tsingy. If our gamble didn't pay off, our predicament would become critical. That was a risk that none of us were ready to take.

I recall being calm but in a state of disbelief as I

pulled out my iridium satellite phone to call for rescue. Despite the odds stacked against us and all the good reasons for calling in a rescue, it felt like quitting. In all of the adventures and expeditions I'd led, including those for missing people, we had never encountered a situation beyond our control, yet here we were, out of food, nearly out of water, and many kilometers away from the only town shown on our map. Fifteen kilometers of tsingy had beaten us and my three-man reconnaissance team sat on a barren hilltop, exhausted and sweating profusely in the heat. Hundreds of "sweat bees" covered our exposed skin, attracted by the salt. We were twenty-nine hours and fifteen hard-fought kilometers from our base camp. Our exit strategy involved at least another eight kilometers of bushwhacking to reach a trail shown on the map, and we would still be twenty kilometers from town. The temperature hovered around 40°C (104°F) and there wasn't a cloud in the sky. We were tired, dehydrated, and hungry; this was a disconcerting expedition first.

Little did we know that our rescue ordeal was just beginning. The first call I made was to Keith, who then called Global Rescue, a provider of emergency extraction insurance for travelers. We quickly learned that despite their assurance that Madagascar had helicopters available for rescue, there were only two that could be accessed in

the entire country, and they were both in use. We also discovered that our situation did not fall under the coverage of our contract; it was considered search and rescue,
which is paid for by the user. In order for them to continue
to help us, they required a pre-payment of $5,000 for any
attempted rescue. After a quick deliberation, Jim provided his credit card number and we awaited our next
update.

In the meantime, the rest of our team had reached the
airstrip and was en route to our camp when Travis got a
hold of them. Updated on the situation by the time they
reached base camp, the team began to explore all the
options available, which, thanks to some political con-
nections, included the Malagasy military (which had
apparently declined Global Rescue's request for assist-
ance). Hours ticked by as the team considered what to
do. Keith had misunderstood our situation and prepped
Tim and Ian to enter the tsingy to rescue us. When we
heard this, we told them in no uncertain terms that doing
so was too risky without a map.

By nightfall, the situation wasn't looking good.
Global Rescue could not access a helicopter and were
talking about air-dropping rations and water from an airplane. Melissa was working on the Malagasy military,
and Keith had Tim and Ian on standby. With no food and
little water remaining, Travis, Jim, and I had a very

serious conversation. Jim thought we should discuss the possibility of continuing south in an attempt to reach the trail to Antsalova.

The batteries in our GPS, satellite phone, and cell phone (which surprisingly worked) were running low so there was a good chance that, once we started, the devices would run out of juice and we'd be entirely out of contact with our base camp and any potential rescuers. If we were going to move, it made the most sense to go at night when it was the coolest and we'd conserve the most energy. We still had juice in our headlamps so we'd be able to see reasonably well. However, if we were wrong and the proposed trail didn't exist or we somehow missed it, we could be walking toward our graves. After discussing the pros and cons, we opted to stay put. At this point, we felt that we had to trust our team to rescue us. It left us feeling helpless because if they failed, we might be too weak to wait another twenty-four hours to make the trek the following night.

In our last communication of the day with our team, they told us to rest up and that they'd update us at first light. Not having planned to overnight in the forest, we had no sleep gear except for an emergency blanket that I had brought in my first aid kit. We slept directly on the red earth; although teeming with biting insects during the day, it was relatively bug-free at night.

We woke before sunrise to the cries of songbirds and awaited our phone call. With Travis's cell phone batteries dead, our Iridium sat phone was our final lifeline. With the power level dangerously low, all calls would have to be quick and concise. Our call came in shortly after daybreak. Melissa had managed to enlist the help of the Malagasy army, which would be dispatching a helicopter to come and get us later that morning. A wave of relief rushed over me.

We set to work making our location visible from the air. Using the shredded remnants of my flimsy survival blanket, we made the site as reflective as possible. We also built a fire, in the hopes that the smoke would attract the pilot's attention. Then we anxiously waited.

The mind does funny things when anticipation and hope are overwhelmingly strong. I strained, listening for the distant sound of a helicopter. The only sounds that morning were the buzzing of sweat bees and the occasional sound of birds. Several times I got excited over the phantom sounds of our rescue, only to be disappointed as they faded to nothing. Around ten o'clock, though, I got the guys' attention. "Listen!" I said. In the distance, the faint whir of a helicopter rotor pierced the buzzing of sweat bees. We strained to follow the sound, fearing that it too would vanish into the forest, and for a moment it did. Then the beating of the rotors intensified and elation swept over me as the helicopter burst into view, flying low and fast over the forest, passing just to the west of us as it traveled north. We jumped, waved, and yelled, our throats parched. Incredibly they did not see us, and it disappeared from sight.

My heart sank, but I sprang to action, snatching up the satellite phone and calling our base camp. With minimal battery life left in the phone and a so-so connection, I had to make my point quickly to Keith: "The helicopter flew over us but didn't see us. Call them and tell them that their coordinates are correct. Don't let them return to the base. We are in the open and waiting for them." Keith confirmed that he would communicate that to the army immediately. I hung up and we waited, swatting at clouds of sweat bees to pass the time.

Bruised ego aside, I knew that we did the right thing in calling for help. There is no shame in surviving, and now we had the rest of the expedition to look forward to. If we'd rolled the dice and decided to self-rescue, we could have very well lucked out, found water, and managed to reach the trail to Antsalova. But it could just have easily gone the other way; with fatigue, failing GPS batteries, a map lacking in critical detail, and a nearly dead satellite phone, we could have perished out there, mere kilometers from a good trail, water, or a village like Bevary.

When the helicopter reappeared thirty minutes later,

we knew it was here to stay, as it hovered over our position looking for a place to land. We put out our campfire, grabbed our gear and the shredded emergency blanket, and briskly walked toward the helicopter, which landed about 200 meters downslope from where we were camped. Two men in olive-green jumpsuits emerged from the chopper and made their way to us. "We're so happy to see you," the pilot said. We laughed and told them that we were even happier to see them. We exchanged handshakes and told them a quick story about our ordeal before lifting off. The pilots were instructed to fly us directly to our base camp, but, after two days on minimal food and water, we asked them to take us to Antsalova, where we could "refuel" on rice and soda.

Seeing the forest from the air was both amazing and frustrating because we realized that we were literally half a kilometer from the savannah to the west and could have handled our own rescue. Despite that, I was at peace with our decision. As the expedition leader, I was responsible for the safety of the team, as well as the overall experience for everyone. If we had denied help in order to push on for selfish, personal reasons, we could have endangered the rest of the team, who might have come looking for us. Explorers must accept certain risks when venturing into uncharted lands. These risks include physical and mental struggles, injury, and even death. Although we acknowledge these as possibilities and try to mitigate against them, I don't think any of us can ever comprehend how fast a situation can turn from good to bad in these environments. Our decision not to honor our agreed-upon turnaround time led us down the rabbit hole, and our situation spiraled rapidly as we pushed further into the unknown. Although we did manage to collect valuable data and get a greater understanding of the environment for the betterment of the project, the cost was putting the whole team in a dangerous position, a mistake I hope to never repeat.

After a day of recovery, we were able to push forward with the expedition and complete what has become one of our most successful projects to date. The team made many exciting discoveries, including of a new cave that we named Anjohibetsara (third largest in the park), a new set of dinosaur tracks east of Antsalova, and an archaeological site containing Vazimba-aged pottery (several hundred years old). We were also able to conduct daily lemur surveys.

While my ego definitely took a major hit from calling in for help, I still maintain that it was the right thing to do given the circumstances. When you are responsible for the welfare of others and the execution of the project, sometimes you have to make humbling decisions that are in the best interest of the group, instead of yourself. Most important, we all got out uninjured and were able to make this a very successful exped- ition. There will always be more projects to tackle, but lives can't be replaced!

12.

Remember What's Important

People always ask why I enjoy pushing myself to oblivion, destroying my body and likely (but hopefully not) taking years off my life because of lack of sleep during these events. They glibly call me crazy, but my answer has always been the same—it's the small things and those "blink and you'll miss it" moments I experience out there that matter most to me. It's a stunning sunrise, a rainbow, a moose or bear unexpectedly popping out of the forest ahead of you, a laugh shared amongst a team of friends in the middle of nowhere, or a group of schoolkids singing your national anthem as you struggle to grasp your paddle with failing hands at the end of an exhausting kayak leg. Those are the moments that stay with you, as vividly as when they happened. Those moments also overshadow the bad and help you forget the suffering. They are what bring you back to the start line, race after race. Adventures and races inherently strip away all of the superfluous trappings in our daily lives and refocus us on what matters most—good relationships, health, food, warmth, and sleep. It's another gift from the sport. When I look at life that way, it seems pretty simple.

With so many races and expeditions under my belt, I've been fortunate to have experienced many such moments, but a few really stick out. One of them occurred in 2001 while racing the RTN Extreme in Corner Brook. Our team was coming into the final stretch of a very long kayak paddle in the open ocean and what happened as we entered the harbor and neared the transition area was one of the most memorable moments of the race for me. It still stirs strong emotions in me to this day. The sun had set an hour or two earlier and we were still holding fourth place and nipping at the heels of the Spanish team, Redbull/ Playstation. We entered Great Triton Harbour with a kilometer left to paddle. I was happy that we'd be leaving the water soon and my numb legs and bum would get moving again. The race organization had been doing a very good job throughout of keeping track of teams. It must have given the small village and the third transition area a heads-up that we were the next team coming in, because there was a surprise waiting for us. A bunch of school-aged children were gathered on a rock outcrop overlooking the water and they were singing "O Canada." It was dark, so at first I could only hear the anthem faintly in the distance, but as our boats sliced through the calm waters of the harbor, the singing grew louder and I was able to make out shapes silhouetted by the moonlight. The large rock outcrop they stood on rose from the water, much like a whale's back. Finally, I was able to make out the individual figures standing on the rock, candles in hand as they sang the sweetest anthem I'd ever heard. It was a magical experience. As we were the first Canadian team through, it was a huge morale booster and brought a lump to my throat and tear to my eye. In a race where you see few teams or spectators, this moment was extremely touching and my heart swelled with pride and gratitude. My life felt totally surreal but utterly amazing. I wouldn't have traded it for anything.

While that experience in Great Triton Harbour was touching, there have been others that are memorable for different reasons, not all of them heart-warming. The Copper Canyon Ultra Marathon and the man at the center of it, Caballo Blanco or Micah True, became an important part of my life around 2010, as I was just entering the world of ultrarunning. I had read the book *Born to Run* and now headed to Mexico with my then-wife Ally to run the race with some ultrarunning friends from my time at McMaster University, Mark Tamminga and Joany Verschuuren. For my first ultra, I definitely picked an anomaly. There is no entry fee, only donations. All racers are encouraged to adopt the name of the spirit animal from which they can draw strength (Mark and Joany named me *el gatto macho*, the tomcat). In addition to a sizable cash prize, the winners get one ton of corn and all finishers receive a voucher for five hundred pounds of corn. Any visitors who find themselves in the money donates their winnings to the Raramuri people. The registration page itself notes that there are "no awards (but self-satisfaction)" and that participants should have "no expectations (but of beauty!)." To enter the race, all hopefuls were required to submit a short essay on why they should be allowed to participate in the event. If your essay convinced Caballo that you were worthy to compete, you'd be allowed to enter but only after agreeing to his infamous waiver, which states, in no uncertain terms, "If I get lost, hurt, or die, it's my own damn fault."

Getting to the start of the race course is a logistical hurdle, too, and once there, racers are expected to pre-hike the entire unmarked race course during the three days leading up to the race. Aid is advertised as limited, so self-sufficiency is a must, and the majority of racers run in rubber sandals, made from discarded tires, with rawhide laces. Despite all this, the race has a growing reputation as a spectacular event that affects runners on a profoundly spiritual level by reminding them about the simplicity of running free, both metaphorically and literally.

Never having competed in an ultra before, I was uncertain whether my experience would qualify me for this gnarly challenge. The gods were smiling (or perhaps frowning) on me and I soon received a note from Caballo welcoming me to the event. I was stoked but also moderately concerned about what I was getting myself into. It was already December and the race was early March—I had less than three months to prepare for my first ultra. To educate myself about Caballo Blanco, I bought the book *Born to Run* by Christopher McDougall. I tore through the pages, absorbing its "shoes are bad" message, which was rippling through the running community at the time. While I don't really consider myself a true runner, I hang out with "real runners" who live to run. For them, this book was an instant sensation that forced them to rethink their running technique and training methods from the feet up. For many, the book proved to be a transformative running bible.

At the center of this saga is a mysterious running messiah named Caballo Blanco and the tire-sandal-wearing Tarahumara Indians, who inhabit Barrancas del Cobre— Mexico's Bermuda Triangle—and are said to be the greatest ultra-distance runners on the planet. The book deals with the spiritual aspect of running and promotes an evolutionary and scientific basis as reason for our need to run free of expensive and scientifically engineered footwear. These theories are tested in a classic fifty-mile showdown between the secretive canyon-dwelling Raramuri Indians and a handful of the United States' best ultrarunners. I was so fascinated by the link between running shoes and injury that I ended up creating an Adventure Science project to explore a similar relationship between core strength and running injuries (we ran the study four months later at the 125 km Canadian Death Race).

The centerpiece of the story, and the most intriguing character, is definitely Caballo Blanco. Meeting Caballo for the first time in person was an experience that ran counter to what I had expected. Tall, tanned, and lanky, he had a face that was creased from years in the sun and his head was now shaved bald. Gone was the wild long hair that I had anticipated. When I quizzed one of his friends about this change, I was told, "The women like him better this way." My first encounter with him was on Grandma Tita's patio (called Paulina's Restaurant in *Born to Run*). I was just finishing a delicious meal of beans, corn, and fresh tortillas when he arrived. I hurriedly rushed to introduce myself and he welcomed me cordially to the town and then introduced me to his ultrarunning girlfriend, Maria, who finalized my registration.

Later that evening I cornered Caballo at a local hostel run by an Oregon transplant named Keith, who maintained an excellent vegetable garden and had high-speed Internet. Caballo had dropped by to visit his old amigo and to sneak a few minutes of Internet time. In this quieter setting, I was pleasantly surprised to find that he had more than a few minutes to chat about the race, the book, and the current state of the union. During our conversation, Caballo spoke candidly about how the book was affecting him in both positive and negative ways. It had apparently raised the ire of the marijuana growers and traffickers in the canyon, who now viewed him as an enemy. He felt that certain individuals featured in the book had profited from the Raramuri without giving back to the people and that some of the information in the book was blatantly untrue. He lamented that his email inbox now overflows with queries from barefoot running converts, wannabes, and more, and that the book read like a giant Vibram commercial. Finally, he noted that, while he loves the race, it was taking up more of his time annually to organize and he didn't know how much longer he would be running it. I appreciated his candor and honesty, and left our conversation with a firm belief that Caballo was indeed strongly committed to the mantra that we should all run free. He was no gimmick.

Standing at the start line on race day, I shivered in the cool morning air. It seemed as though the entire town was out to watch the festivities; spectators mixed with dozens of machine gun–toting soldiers. The Raramuri were clustered on the start line. Men wore their sleeveless cotton race jerseys, trademark huarache sandals, and everything from traditional skirts to shorts and jeans. Women wore brightly colored ankle-length skirts and blouses, and plastic sandals. The *extranjeros* (foreigners), as they called us, were mostly clothed in high-tech wicking fabric, and all but one wore trail runners.

To my surprise, the race started on time at 6:30 a.m., and in stark contrast to the pomp and ceremony that preceded the bib pickup the previous evening, the race began with barely a whisper. There was only the quiet countdown by Caballo. My cue to start racing was the sudden surge forward of the Raramuri. The pace was fast as we coursed through the main street toward the edge of town, urged on by the cheering spectators. Over 350 athletes from Mexico, Canada, the US, and Europe were finally running free.

The race course remained largely as it was described in *Born to Run*. It was a Y-shaped route of gravel road and single track. Racers were required to check in to each turnaround point on the race course by stating their number (in my case, *dos ciento nuevo*, or two fingers, fist, nine fingers) and receiving a colored wristband—four in total. In the cool morning air, my running felt light and easy. I was enjoying the experience for what it was—a collection of athletes from all walks of life were there to celebrate the simple joys of running long distances in beautiful places. As the miles ticked by, I ran with a smile on my face and felt that I was shadowing the Raramuri way of life.

As the race progressed and the heat of the day settled in, I began to struggle and that light, easy feeling gave way to an ugly walk-run as my legs became cramp factories, but I pushed forward, reaching the finish line after 9:04:35, and in fortieth place. While the race wasn't quite as extreme as the book had described, it did live up to Caballo's claims of beauty and self-satisfaction. Although competitive, this race is as much a pilgrimage and a spiritual journey as it is a test of endurance. As I reflected on the experience over the following days, these elements rose as the most important ones—not my finishing time or rank. In some races, you put your head down and end up seeing red until you cross the finish line, while in other races, you keep your head up, your pulse steady, and just take in the experience for what it is.

The race opened my eyes to the capacity we all have to run long distances and gave me a greater appreciation of running free. *Korima* (giving without expectation) flowed freely during the event, from competitor to competitor and from volunteer to competitor. More than once I handed out gels or salt tablets to amigos I passed on the course. More than once the volunteers helped me with massage. It is fair to say, though, that this race is unique. Here, we race to help others preserve a culture we all believe in—economically, through our entry fees and our corn and bean donations post-race, and culturally, through opening our minds to gain some level of under-standing of the Raramuri people and the respect for their traditions. Caballo's message is that by running free in places like Copper Canyon, we remind ourselves about the importance of peace, harmony, and sharing in our lives, and perhaps make time without distraction to appre-ciate all we have. I think he's bang on. I try to carry this perspective into all of my races, adventures, and through my day-to-day so that I don't forget about what should be key priorities—health, happiness, relationships, and an appreciation of and respect for our planet and those we share it with.

Even after the race was over, Caballo Blanco was someone I thought of often during the following years and, in fact, our paths would cross again in 2012.

If you ask a baby boomer where they were when Kennedy was assassinated, or when Apollo 11 put Neil Armstrong and Buzz Aldrin on the moon, they will likely have an instant recollection. The moment I learned that Caballo Blanco had gone missing is one of those strong memories for me. I was training on my bike in my base-ment when I heard the news. I recall that moment like it was yesterday.

Caballo had disappeared while out for a solo trail run in the Gila Wilderness Area of New Mexico on the morn-ing of Tuesday, March 27, 2012. He was spending a few days with his friends Dan and Jane Brumner at their lodge, and they reported him missing on Wednesday morning when he had not returned. By Thursday, the media got hold of the story. Messages were quickly pouring online with runners sending their "hopes and prayers" that he would be found alive, and soon. Those messages, as well meaning as they were, made me angry. *Hopes and prayers aren't going to find him; boots on the ground will,* I thought to myself and made the decision that I was going to use the skills I'd gained through the previous years of Adventure Science searches to go down to New Mexico and find him. I wasn't going alone, though, and within an hour Tim Puetz, a good friend whom I had met in Mexico two years earlier, and another ultrarunner named Caleb Wilson had committed to meet me in Phoenix the following day. The next morning I told my boss that I needed the rest of the day off and by noon I was on an airplane.

The three of us connected at Sky Harbor Airport in Phoenix, hopped into our rental car, and drove through the night to reach the remote Gila Cliff Dwellings National Monument. We arrived at 4:30 a.m. and laid our air mattresses on the warm asphalt of the park service office and dozed off. Nearly four and a half hours after sunrise we were finally paired with a trained search-and-rescue team from Las Cruces, New Mexico. We spent the better part of the first day plodding slowly through a dusty, trail-less area that wasn't all that inviting for a runner. But, in the name of thoroughness, we played along and examined every fragmentary footprint, broken branch, and fabric patch we saw. Considering that our ultrarunning friends Jamil and Kahlil Couray had searched the same area the day before, we felt redundant as we crawled along. The day moved at a glacial pace due in part to the heat and in part to the general lack of fitness. By the time we wrapped up our search, it was after three in the afternoon and we hadn't found anything. We slowly made our way back to the ranger station—we were down but not out.

Most of the search teams had returned by the time we reached the ranger station. It was after four, and there were no new clues. Helicopters and fixed-wing aircraft still flew overhead, but the official search was basically wrapped up for the day. However, with a few hours of light remaining, we knew we still had time to search on our own. The three of us had traveled too far to stop after only six hours of searching; we were prepared to go rogue and decided to spend the remaining hours of sunlight running one of Caballo's favorite trails. If he was going to be rescued, it needed to be soon. He had already been missing for four days. Humans can survive for weeks without food, but when outdoors and exposed to the elements we don't normally survive more than three to four days. We were frustrated and had less than twenty-four hours to find our friend before we had to catch our flights. It was time to start thinking like a trail runner and use the search experience we'd gained through Adventure Science.

We decided to try our luck in an area near the famous Gila Cliff Dwellings that Caballo had apparently been fond of visiting. In addition, they were on a well-established hiking trail that could easily be a 12-mile loop from his starting point. For whatever reason, the search efforts were not focused in this area and the coverage had been light. We had been running for nearly thirty minutes when Tim spotted two runners, Ray Molina and Jessica Haines, coming toward us, out of breath. "We found him," Ray said. "He's dead, and he's lying in the creek . . . on his back." I was stunned. The creek he was referring to was named Little Creek and lay two miles uphill from where we stood. The rest of the conversation was a blur. Tim and I felt compelled to head to Caballo's resting place to help with the recovery and to watch over the body if search-and rescue was unable to airlift him that night. We were carrying nothing more than the shirts on our back, so after a quick hand-off of maps, some food, and a few pieces of gear, Tim and I bolted up the trail, while the others continued on to the ranger station to report the sad news.

We intersected Little Creek, which was fed by icy meltwater from the snowcapped peaks looming high above. It wasn't more than thigh deep at its deepest point and didn't have a strong current. It was actually relatively easy to run down, although we quickly discovered that the submerged boulders were very slick. We discovered Caballo one and a half miles downstream. He was lying peacefully on his back—his legs in the water, torso out. His water bottle bobbed next to him in the creek. This was the first dead body I had ever seen—and oddly, I wasn't frightened. His body didn't seem real to me. His skin was waxy and pale. He had blue bruises on his knees and one finger, so it looked to us as though he had fallen at some point, most likely while in the stream. Judging by the position of his body, though, I think that he just sat down to ice his legs and then lay down, so he likely passed away on Tuesday. The autopsy report suggests arrhythmia ultimately felled him, brought on by heart disease, which ran in the family.

After finding him and spending a few silent minutes with our own thoughts, Tim and I got to work to prepare to spend the night. As we worked, I thought about my own mortality, but mostly I reflected on my experiences with Caballo, who was different things to different people. I really didn't know him that well but appreciated and respected him for championing the Raramuri and opening their culture, and that of ultrarunning, to me and the world. For that, I felt that I had a debt to repay, which was maybe why I felt compelled to join the search for him.

I was sad, not because of his death but because of the loss of the potential he represented. We spent the next few hours huddled close to the fire, as the daytime temperature of over 30°C (86°F) plummeted toward freezing at a nearly 2,000-meter altitude. Around midnight the first recovery team had arrived. The team brought extra clothing, as well as food, a stove, and coffee that made the night go by a lot easier than it would have with the two of us sharing the emergency blanket! Exhausted, I drifted in and out of sleep for the rest of the night, listening to Ray's nonstop storytelling about Copper Canyon, Caballo, and the good times they used to have.

Being a guru had presented opportunities for Caballo to share his story as disciples sought his counsel on how to run free both metaphorically and literally. He had recently completed a speaking tour in Europe, and his agent, Scott, likened him traveling abroad to Crocodile Dundee. Caballo had truly enjoyed the experience, and they were planning a follow-up trip. He was honestly floored that, in London, over three hundred anxious fans lined up to see him. There was a documentary film being shot, as well as a major motion picture in the works. His star was about to glow even brighter. Despite this, he still remained a champion for the Raramuri and had run his most successful race to date just weeks prior to his death.

Ultimately, Caballo was beginning to realize that he had the ability to inspire others through his words and actions. And while it might have taken a book and legions of fans to convince him, he had been doing it for those he loved through it all, without realizing it. His girlfriend, Maria Walton, shared with me the most poignant example of this when she recounted an experience she shared with him during her first 100-mile running race:

"Micah's strength, endurance, and persistence challenged me to reach goals I thought were unachievable. In 2010, he paced me for my first 100-mile race. At mile 97, I was very weak and uncertain if I could continue. He gently reached out his hand and said, 'Hey, *mariposa amor de miel* (my darling, loving butterfly), give me your hand, honey. We can make this final climb together.' I began crying and acknowledged that I was certain he would never pace me in a race again, since I was so emotional. He tenderly stated, 'You're right, honey. I won't. Because I love you too much to ever see you in this much pain again. And the last time I ran some guy in for the final miles of his ultra, it ended up in a goddamned book.'"

For a long time, I thought that his legacy was his fifty-mile ultramarathon, but now I realize that it is his genuine appreciation for what he valued and those he loved in life. This is the life lesson that he would have shared with us all. Even without all the conventional trappings of wealth,

Caballo Blanco died a rich man. As someone with multiple interests, I often find myself easily distracted by life's daily noise—bills to pay, work to do, etc. But because of these and similar experiences, I now work much harder to make time for what really matters to me, those things in life that bring me overflowing happiness, freedom, love, and appreciation for where I live. Although I like to have high-quality gear and stay in nice places when I travel, I've found that they don't make me happy over the long term— it's the experiences that I have and the moments I share with people that make the biggest difference in my life.

Ultras for Everyone

In North America, because many of us have very comfortable lives, we tend to settle into a routine and do not strive to reach our potential mentally, physically, and emotionally. I firmly believe that everyone should run at least one ultramarathon in their life. Humans thrive on challenges, which inspire our biggest innovations. Our bodies are designed to be highly efficient over long distances. Whether you believe that you are a runner or not, we all are built to run at least a few kilometers at a time. Running not only improves your fitness but it enhances your mental health as well, releasing endorphins into your system that produce the often-mentioned "runner's high." Competing in an ultra doesn't mean running every step—not even the best in the world do that. Run as much as you can and walk the rest. In ultras, most athletes walk the climbs and run the flats and descents. Training for an ultra will add focus and motivation to your day, and, with dedication, improvement usually comes rapidly. The race itself will provide a roller-coaster ride of emotional highs and lows, challenging you many times over. Persevering to the finish line, regardless of pace, will give you a long-lasting sense of achievement and, perhaps more important, a greater perspective on managing stress in your daily life. Ultras have helped me train my ability to ride out difficult moments in business and life with the understanding that what goes up must come down, and vice versa.

Blood, Sweat, and Airplanes

An Adventure Athlete's Travel Log

For me, studying maps unlocks my imagination, letting loose my wonderment. When selecting races to compete in for *Boundless* or expeditions for Adventure Science, I typically start by looking at a map and asking myself, "Where do I want to go next?" or "What country looks intriguing?" Although I've described numerous races and adventures in the book, in this section you'll find descriptions of all the *Boundless* races and Adventure Science projects, as well as my favorite other races and adventures. This will give context to the stories and also help set your imagination free, so you too can ask yourself, "Where will I go next?"

ADVENTURE SCIENCE

2008: Bridgeport, Nevada—The Search for Steve Fossett
As the search for missing pilot Steve Fossett unfolded in the arid mountains of Nevada and California, I started to

think about putting a team of athletes on the ground in the remote and heavily forested parts of the search area. Ten months later, I led a ten-person team through those mountains. We didn't find him, but we were the closest of all independent search teams to doing so (he was found indirectly by a hiker near Mammoth Lakes, California, several months later), and the project served to validate the Adventure Science concept.

2009: Sedona, Arizona—The Search for N2700Q
Building on our first airplane search, we teamed up with a larger group led by airplane search ace Chris Killian to search for this missing Cessna near Sedona, Arizona. The airplane was discovered after we asked the US Forest Service if any fires were reported the day the plane vanished. As it turned out, several hikers had not only seen a fire deep in the canyon but also photographed it—though they didn't know it was the wreck, still only a few hours old.

2009: Bruce Trail, Ontario—Blaze
After hiking sections of the Bruce Trail as a child, I was intrigued by this 900 km trail that runs through southern Ontario. With the help of researcher Dr. Mark Tarnopolsky of McMaster University, I built two teams to battle head to head on the course while at the same time contributing to a study that would help us better understand the

muscle damage that occurred during ultrarunning—a novel study at the time. We also shattered the existing team fastest-known-time record in the process and still hold it today with our sub-four-day time.

2010: Grande Cache, Alberta—Go Death Racer

The Canadian Death Race is one of the most popular ultras in Canada, partly because of its longevity but also because of its remote and rugged nature. This was my first big ultra, and I enjoyed the challenge, but it's not an ultra I'd do again—unfortunately, I just didn't feel that the value or community support was up there with other races I've done. It was also the subject of my first documentary, a film called *Go Death Racer*, which was where the concept for *Boundless* came from.

2010: Bishop, California—The Search for Lieutenant Steeves's Missing USAF Lockheed T-33 Jet

This was my first project in the field with Chris Killian. We traveled to the thirteen-thousand-foot Palisade Glacier in California to track down a lead gleaned from a master's of science study, which identified hydrocarbons in an alpine stream originating in the area. Our theory was that a wrecked jet may have been the point source of the hydrocarbons. After spending several days traversing the glacier and exploring the ramparts surrounding it, we were chased to the valley by bad weather—but felt confident that the glacier did not contain the wrecked I-33.

2011: Musandam, Oman (Khasab)—Beyond Roads

This project started as an extension of the work I had done on tsunamis for my PhD but morphed into a joint tsunami-archaeology project based on initial research I conducted on this forgotten part of Oman. Roadless and poorly studied, this region is rife with difficult-to-access ancient archaeological sites scattered through the mountains. Despite the challenges of exploring a roadless and mapless area, we learned a lot, discovered many incredible sites, and still are just scratching the surface of this beautiful part of the world. We had the honor of carrying an Explorers Club flag on this project.

2012: Gila National Forest, New Mexico—The Search for Caballo Blanco

This impromptu project took Tim Puetz, Caleb Wilson, and me deep into the heart of the Gila National Forest. We ended up spending the night alongside Caballo Blanco's body and learned how to search for missing people. This project was unique in that government officials were good enough to invite civilian help but unable to run an efficient search—extremely frustrating when time was of the essence.

2012: Great Falls, Montana—Caves of Montana
This project was created in an effort to enhance the team's rope skills, which would allow for greater capacity on future projects. Knowing that the region around Great Falls is rife with caves, both known and unknown, we opted to spend several days in this region, exploring. We discovered and explored several caves in the process. The caves in the area tended to exist as vertical sinks, rather than as lateral passages.

2013: Medora, North Dakota—100 Miles of Wild: North Dakota Badlands Transect
With the rapid expansion of oil drilling in the Bakken Formation, Dr. Richard Rothaus and I had a long-standing interest in this region, his from an archaeological and mine from a geological and hydrocarbon production perspective. We had two-person teams trek three routes daily as we made our way south along the Little Missouri River, exploring this wild and remote area to better understand the effect drilling was having here. We examined well pads for spills, looked for litter, monitored wildlife, and recorded any paleontological or archaeological discoveries, of which there were several, the most significant being bone beds containing mostly bison. We were again awarded an Explorers Club flag for this project.

2014: Great Tsingy, Madagascar—100 Miles of Wild:
Madagascar's Limestone Labyrinth
When it takes you three days to drive some two hundred kilometers to reach your base camp, you know you're off the grid. Madagascar is a nation with minimal infrastructure and social services outside its capital. This place is so underexplored that, in one week, we managed to find the third-largest known cave system in the park, a new archaeological site, and the most northerly dinosaur tracks in the country. The National Parks service was both extremely interested in and very grateful for our findings and report, which provided it with the first documentation for what that part of this dangerous stone forest contained. In addition, we conducted daily lemur surveys, and Jim Mandelli, Travis Steffens, and I were also the first Westerners (possibly first ever) to traverse this portion of the park. Having left our field research station, we were forced to beat a hasty exit from the town of Antsalova on our final day there to avoid witnessing the public execution of a cattle thief captured the previous evening. We carried an Explorers Club flag during this project.

2014: Bishop, California—The Search for Lieutenant
Steeves's Missing USAF Lockheed T-33 Jet 2
Digging deep into the details of this remarkable survival story, we embarked on a comprehensive mathematical

analysis to determine our search area. Armed with possible trajectories for equipment jettisoned from Steeves's jet, a large team of athletes joined me in searching targets in the Kings Canyon of the Sierra Nevada. Although nothing related to the Steeves search was located, the team did find several other objects that until then had gone unidentified—reported by pilots in the past but never confirmed on the ground.

2015: Tahoe, California—Fossett Files: In Search of Lost Airplanes in the Sierra Nevada
Steve Fossett's disappearance in 2007 launched the largest search-and-rescue effort in US history and in the process delivered a number of unidentified wreck sites spotted from the air but not explored on the ground because the wreck did not match the plane Fossett was flying that day. The wrecks spotted were cross-referenced to existing data-bases but could not be validated. These sightings ranged from mostly intact planes to mere glints of metal or glass. With a team of very fit athletes, we groundtruthed a hand-ful of these sites and were able to confirm them as known wrecks—and not undiscovered.

2015: Tobermory, Ontario—The Ghosts of Tobermory: An Amphibious Exploration of Fathom Five Marine Park
Going back to the start of our Blaze project, this was our first aquatic project and more of a proof-of-concept test than

rank exploration. Using inflatable Jimmy Lewis stand up paddleboards, we paddled to a number of wrecks from the late 1800s. We were entirely self-supported, and camped and paddled the area over the course of a few days, snorkeling all wreck sites.

2016: Musandam, Oman (Khasab)—Beyond Roads 2
A white whale of sorts, completing a traverse of this difficult ridgeline is a must-do before I die. This project was a follow-up to our abbreviated 2011 effort. We knew there were more sites to discover in the highlands and still had a significant amount of terrain to cover to complete the trek. Armed with our learnings about the region, we returned with a high-powered team of athletes, only to be stopped seven days into our nine-day push after Jim broke his ankle when a boulder fell away under him. Because of the emergency evacuation, there are still two food and water caches out there for explorers to stumble across in the future. We are currently in the midst of planning our third and hopefully final trip there.

BOUNDLESS SEASON ONE:
FILMED JULY–DECEMBER 2012

July: Molokai, Hawaii—Molokai 2 Oahu Stand Up Paddleboard (52 km)
This is the world championships for paddleboarding and

has become the de facto world championship for long distance stand up paddleboard racing. We went into it overconfident and unprepared and came out humbled men (disqualified for kneeling). It is an incredible event for seasoned open-water paddlers and definitely not suitable for novice athletes.

August: Akureyri, Iceland—Fire and Ice Ultra (250 km)
Turbo (aka Paul Trebilcock) and I raced the inaugural version of this marathon and therefore raced a small field (finishing first place). This was my first stage-running race and because of a family wedding, I reached the start line in central Iceland less than four hours before the 8 a.m. start. Despite the unseasonably cold weather, it was an incredible event in a little-traveled part of the world, and I give it top marks for scenery and organization.

September: Kimanjo, Kenya—Amazing Maasai Marathon (75 km)
This route is entirely on the dirt roads of Kenya's Laikipia County. Organized as a charity run, this event supports the education of girls in the region. The route is hilly and the temperature will be hot, so heat acclimation is an important consideration. You'll be racing local Kenyans (I was the first Western finisher that year), so don't expect to win. The highlight for me was running with so many

young schoolchildren, who ran effortlessly and with big bright smiles for their half or full marathon.

October: Cradock, South Africa—Hansa Fish River Canoe Marathon (80 km)

This race was like the Super Bowl of paddling and is a must for any skilled marathon paddler. The usually placid Great Fish River becomes a raging torrent one week of the year when the sleepy farming community of Cradock comes to life to host one of the largest paddling races in the world. The paddling and competition is first rate and the afterparty each night is even better. This was one of my favorite races, despite our lack of paddling acumen in season one. (Despite enduring a brutal day on the water and a Did Not Finish on day one, we paddled with experienced paddlers on day two and finished respectably.)

October: Hurricane, Utah—6 Hours in Frog Hollow MTB (80 km)

This race wasn't on the original schedule, but as we started to feel the effects of so much racing, our producer, Steven Bray, scrambled to find a bike race to throw in to help us (me) recover. The race is pretty quirky, but it is competitive, and the course is fast, fun, and flowy—all the things a mountain bike trail should be. Turbo had a great race here despite a crash that left him with a bloodied face. I fell victim to leg cramps and watched my hopes of a strong finish vanish.

October: Faiyum, Egypt—4 Deserts Sahara Race (250 km)
I was nervous going into this race because of the patellar tendinitis that had limited my effort in Kenya several weeks earlier, but thankfully I ran the entire distance without it bothering me, finishing second place. Although expensive to enter, the 4 Deserts series is a world-class set of races with excellent race support, a competitive field, and stunning race courses. This is without a doubt one of the toughest events I've ever competed in, because of the heat. Heat training is a must in preparing for this race.

November: Siem Reap, Cambodia—Ancient Khmer Path (200 km)
Best known as the episode in which Sophie nearly died from hyponatremia, this ultra marathon was interesting from a cultural perspective, but the race course disappointed me. Instead of racing on narrow jungle trails for a week, we raced on rural roads in the baking sun most days, and the humidity made sleeping in our tents difficult. Despite this, we did see incredible archaeological sites, pass innumerable smiling children and locals, and experience a region of Cambodia that few tourists see.

December: Phuket, Thailand—Ironman 70.3 (113 km)

The capstone to an incredible four months of racing, my first triathlon was a wonderful experience. We stayed in the beautiful resort of Laguna Phuket and were treated to a challenging and interesting race course, the highlights being a saltwater and freshwater swim and a hilly bike course. Note that this is no longer an Ironman event, having been added to the Challenge series (a popular European-run global triathlon series).

Season One Total: 8 races; 19 weeks; 1,060 km made of 1,100 km attempted

Season One Medal Count: 1 win, 1 second-place finish

BOUNDLESS SEASON TWO:
FILMED JULY 2013–MARCH 2014

July: Bad Goisern, Austria—Salzkammergut Trophy (220 km)

This brutally tough mountain bike race is one of my favorite *Boundless* races to date. Despite breaking a bone in my foot several days before the event, I enjoyed almost every minute of the mountainous route. Definitely skewed toward double-track riding, this is a less technical race course compared with other European marathon mountain bike courses. There are shorter distances available for those who want to work up to the full 220 kilometers.

August: Lake Khövsgöl, Mongolia—Sunrise to Sunset, aka
Most Beautiful Ultra (100 km)
What struck me most about Mongolia was the lack of
fences. From the air, the country around the race was an
unbroken expanse of steppe and boreal forests. Our rus-
tic accommodations on the shore of the majestic Lake
Khövsgöl were enjoyable, though I felt like we didn't get
enough to eat each day leading up to the race. The course
was indeed beautiful and included a good mix of trails
and roads. (I won the marathon but withdrew from the
100 km race because of knee pain, despite leading at the
time.) Athletes will have an opportunity to get to know
each other well in advance of the event, as it is a small
field, and everyone travels in together (be prepared for
the insane traffic of Ulaanbaatar).

August: Fort William, Scotland—Ramsay's Round (103 km)
Many races are proclaimed as the most difficult in all the
land, whereas some sneak up on you quietly and bring you
to your knees. This twenty-four-hour challenge is definitely
just that. You have twenty-four hours (well, for me, it took
twenty-seven) to navigate twenty-four difficult Munros
(peaks over three thousand feet), including Ben Nevis
(tallest in the UK), on an unmarked route. I dealt with bad
weather, incredibly slippery conditions, gale-force winds,
and brutally thick fog. I called it one of the worst weather

days that I had ever had the pleasure to be outside in. The Scots I was running with called it a Saturday in August.

September: Leeuwarden, the Netherlands—Stand Up Paddleboard 11 City Tour (220 km)

This is a very cool race. Turbo and I took this on a mere three days after Ramsay's Round, I was impressed by the canal system of northern Holland. This course follows the classic route of the Elfstedentocht skate race, taking athletes through a series of canals and lakes over the 220 km distance. The rural scenery is tranquil, and the old cities and towns are beautiful. This is a well-organized event that even a week of steady rain couldn't tarnish.

September: Iquitos, Peru—Amazing Amazon Raft Race (160 km)

I fondly refer to this race as the most surprisingly difficult race I've ever competed in (achieving a second-place finish in the international category). Good luck getting information about this event online—it's more of a locals-only challenge, much like the Barkley marathon used to be. Teams of four build rafts out of logs supplied by the race organizers and then paddle for three days down the Amazon River to the city of Iquitos. Although a booze cruise for some, there is surprisingly good prize money, which makes it three days of hell for the teams at the front in the slow-moving chocolate milk they call the Amazon. There is also the added bonus of a laser-light dance party every night.

October: Santa Clarita, California—Furnace Creek 508 (568 km)

This classic ultra-endurance road bike race, which travels from Los Angeles, through Death Valley, and ends in Palm Springs, was unfortunately shortened to 568 kilometers (from 508 miles to 353) the year we competed. The route was hilly, and the wind was in my face for most of the ride. This is one of those races where you see how much mental grit you've got in the bank. No drafting and more than twenty hours of saddle time will repeatedly test your desire to reach the finish. This race capped an intensive month of racing and basically broke Turbo and me. We canceled an event in India slated for late October and took November off to try to recover. Because of new restrictions on riding through Death Valley, this race has since moved to Nevada.

December: San José, Costa Rica—Adventure Racing World Championships (700 km)

The AR World Champs move host sites annually, and it was our bad luck to catch the Costa Rican addition. Advertised as some seven hundred kilometers long, this was a true sufferfest. Granted, we did see some amazing sights as we traveled through dense mangroves, across mountains that touched the clouds, and through virgin jungle, but this race took us to our breaking point.

February: Whitehorse, Yukon—Yukon Arctic Ultra (160 km)
This is one of the classic winter ultras, drawing an especially hardy breed of athlete to Whitehorse every year to take on one of several distances of up to almost seven hundred kilometers. Athletes can race on foot, fat bike, or cross-country skis. It truly is a wilderness race, with checkpoints located fifty kilometers apart, so self-sufficiency is a must. Despite the surprisingly high entry fee, this is a no-frills race. The finish lines are not glamorous, there is no prizing, and there is minimal fanfare. There is, however, plenty of remote Canadian wilderness to be explored. (I finished third place overall and was the first person to complete the cross-country ski on first attempt.)

March: Urique, Mexico—Copper Canyon Ultra Marathon (80 km)
This was my first ultra and, as such, holds a special place in my heart. It is a community-supported event that takes athletes through the beautiful Copper Canyon of Mexico. It is well marked and well supported with aid stations and lots of spectators. I like to think of this as ground zero for ultrarunning in North America, since the race is based on

the concept of giving back. This race is currently on hold because of drug violence in the area.

Season Two Total: 9 races; 35 weeks; 1,903 km made of 2,311 km attempted
Season Two Medal Count: 1 win, 1 second-place finish, 1 third-place finish

BOUNDLESS SEASON THREE: FILMED FEBRUARY–OCTOBER 2015

February: Oracle, Arizona—24 Hours in the Old Pueblo (270 km)

For the first race with a beefed-up cast, I was pleasantly surprised by this massive twenty-four-hour bike race. The atmosphere is electric, and it is aptly described as the Woodstock of mountain bike races. The race loop, just over twenty-five kilometers, consists of rolling hills, steady climbs, and flowy single track. It sadly doubles as the annual kangaroo-rat slaughter, as hundreds of these rats are hit and killed by cyclists during the event, after being attracted to the bike lights on the course. It was a fourth-place finish for Hunter McIntyre and me in this race.

March: Sisimiut, Greenland—Arctic Circle Race (160 km)

This epic cross-country ski race, occurring north of the

Arctic Circle in Greenland, is hosted with pride by the community of Sisimiut. The route is incredibly well groomed despite its remoteness, with grooming machines track setting each night for the next day's ski. Athletes can expect all types of weather—we experienced thick fog, which made it incredibly difficult to see the track because of the complete lack of vegetation on the route. (In fact, day three was canceled because of the weather.) You will be skiing through a mountainous landscape with unsurpassed natural beauty but plenty of challenging terrain.

April: San Pedro de Atacama, Chile—Atacama Extreme (160 km)
This 160 km race takes runners through the heart of the Atacama Desert—the driest non-polar desert in the world. Participating in only its second running (the first was cut short by a sandstorm), we followed a flatter route than I had anticipated—challenging athletes with endless roads and salt flats instead of treating us to the flanks of the surrounding snowcapped peaks. Perhaps it was the fact that we were already at eight thousand feet to begin with. Despite this and some poor on-course markings, it was a fun event with a great atmosphere. The race highlight was definitely the semi-feral dogs that followed us during the event, one even sticking with Turbo for more than fifty kilometers of the race! I finished third overall.

May: Moab, Utah—Adventure Xstream (80 km)

I was nervous about returning to adventure racing after our experience in Costa Rica, but this race turned out to be a ton of fun. This is a mountain biker's race course, with the trekking and running being relatively short. There is a massive rappel in the middle of it, and a mediocre paddle down the Colorado River to finish the event. The navigation is generally straightforward (despite two navigational bobbles of mine) and the level of competition is high, so fast teams will be in good company. Our team placed second.

June: Vail, Colorado—GoPro Mountain Games Ultimate Mountain Challenge (70 km)

The Mountain Games are a long-lived tradition in Colorado, and we chose to take on all of the toughest events, including a whitewater downriver stand up paddleboard, mountain bike race, 10 km trail running race, and a road bike time trial. This is a fun weekend, and the town balloons in size thanks to the spectators and athletes. If you're a focused and competitive athlete in the Ultimate Mountain Challenge, you'll miss out on some great parties, but if you're just there for fun, it's bound to be an awesome weekend.

July: Combloux, France—MB Race Culture Vélo (140 km)

Advertised as a brutally difficult mountain bike race, this

one is true to its word. The first hour of riding is fairly gentle, climbing paved and gravel roads in the Alps. This doesn't last, and the relentless climbing, difficult single track, and hot temperatures eventually add up to make it a challenging day in the saddle. Although I didn't have a great race (dropping out at seventy kilometers), the event is top-notch. The route is well marked, the organizers are highly accommodating, and the course will test even the best. There are three lengths within the event—70, 100, and 140 kilometers—so if you're not feeling it on race day, you can bow out with some grace at one of the earlier marks.

July: Aberfeldy, Scotland—Artemis Great Kindrochit Quadrathlon (90 km)
I entered this race with my tail between my legs after withdrawing early the previous weekend from the MB Race Culture Vélo in France but was rewarded with one of the best races of my life (finishing third place). This two-person race includes a 1.5 km swim across the loch, followed by a 25 km run across seven Munros, a 12 km kayak paddle, and a 50 km ride around the loch. It's a classic Scottish challenge, with variable weather and hearty participants. And it's a very well organized event with a strong field, great race course, unique finish line (think *Braveheart*), and fun after-party.

August: Wiarton, Ontario—Bruce Peninsula Multisport Race (100 km)

Run by a friend of mine, this event has been growing in popularity over the past few years, attended primarily by athletes living near Toronto. The race includes a beautiful paddle around an island, followed by a series of mountain biking and trail running legs. It's a well-thought-out course that requires both technical skills (riding and running on very rocky trails) and flat-out horsepower for the open roads. The trail markings need to improve, but otherwise it's a well-done event showcasing a beautiful region. Rory Bosio and I won the coed category in a record time, almost catching Turbo and Hunter at the line.

September: Stockholm, Sweden—Ötillö (75 km)

This is both ground zero for and the world championships of swimrun—a sport that is storming the globe. Created on a drunken bet, the event is now ten years old and each year draws—for a mere 130 spots—over fifteen hundred applicants, all with the goal to swim and run across the 75 km course and twenty-five islands. I raced with Hunter McIntyre, and after a rocky start (he was a much stronger swimmer) we settled into a rhythm and finished in the middle of the pack. This race is highly focused on safety, well organized, and incredibly fun—despite the cold water and big waves.

October: Tahoe, California—Spartan World Championship (?? km)

After competing in the ultra-beast the previous year, I was looking forward to testing myself on the shorter course, and with the best Spartan racers on the planet. The course was as advertised: tough. In addition to difficult obstacles, there was significant climbing (at elevation) in this event. Highlights included a sandbag carry at the highest point on the course, and a sustained downhill run later in the race. I struggled with the hoist, and got chilled to the bone on a swim through a snowmaking pond just below the alpine terrain. If you like obstacle course races and are looking for one that will test all your muscles (not just your heart), consider this one, if you don't mind burpees.

Season Three Total: 10 races; 36 weeks; 1,057 km made of 1,167 km attempted

Season Three Medal Count: 1 win, 1 second-place finish, 2 third-place finishes, 1 fourth-place finish

MY FAVORITE BLISTER MAKERS

BEST ADVENTURE RACE

Eco-Challenge (2001)—Queenstown, New Zealand

For me, this was like going to the Olympics. The race took

teams through the mountains of the Mount Cook Range on New Zealand's South Island. It lived up to its reputation as the pinnacle of adventure racing at the time and is still one of my greatest racing experiences. Mark Burnett knows how to put on an event, and it's a shame that the Eco-Challenge is no more.

FUN TWENTY-FOUR-HOUR CHALLENGE

Maui Wowie (2016)—Maui, Hawaii

After visiting Maui in season one of *Boundless*, I knew I had to go back to explore the island my way—via a long, hard day. I created the Maui Wowie (now part of an invitation-only series called The Wowie; visit www.gowowie.com). This sea–summit–sea challenge saw Hunter, Rory Bosio, Max Wilcox, and I start at the ocean near Paia, ride to the top of the Haleakala volcano (over ten thousand feet), run a 27 km lap inside the crater, and then mountain bike down the back of the volcano on trails before returning to our starting point—a first of its kind, to the best of our knowledge.

BEST RACE

Tor des Géants (2011)—Courmayeur, Italy

This 330 km mountain run is a beast of epic proportions. Even though I withdrew after about 170 kilometers into the race with an injury, this is still one of the greatest races I've ever participated in. The organizers and volunteers pour their hearts and souls into making the event challenging and memorable. From an insanely beautiful and demanding race course to first-class aid stations and life bases, this race caters to the athlete. For hammerheads like me, the goal is to finish in around four days. For everyone else, you've got seven days to run or run-walk through the Italian Alps while still managing a solid sleep each night.

CANADIAN CLASSIC

Canadian Death Race (2010)—Grande Cache, Alberta
This is the Canadian classic as far as mountain ultras go. One of the oldest, it takes runners on a 125 km loop from the coal mining town of Grande Cache. Despite the town's initial skepticism, this is now the biggest event for the region annually. Expect a sellout for both team and solo spots most years. The race boasts enthusiast participants, great volunteers, and a challenging course, with great views from the top of Mount Hamel.

STELLAR MOUNTAIN RUNNING

Transalpine-Run (2016)—Garmisch-Partenkirchen, Germany
Despite a language barrier for me at the event and some challenges with the organizers, I can't deny this as a first-class trail running race, stretching from Germany to Italy

via Austria. The race includes an abundance of single track, has well-stocked aid stations, and incorporates the best scenery of the area. Accommodations are the athlete's responsibility, and it's as inclusive as you would want it to be. It's a much more serious race than its sister event— the TransRockies Run in Colorado, so it doesn't have the summer-camp-for-adults feel, but as far as trail races go, you'll be hard-pressed to find better mountain trails to run.

BEST-KEPT SECRET
Catalina Island, California
I traveled here in 2015 for a training weekend with Hunter and was impressed by the incredible trail system running the length of the island. The trail network easily allowed me to accumulate more than eighty kilometers of running in two days. Accommodations exist across the island, which is also popular for camping and exploring remote beaches, and just a short ferry ride from Los Angeles.

MY FAVORITE FKT (FASTEST-KNOWN TIME)
Mount Rundle, Canmore, Alberta
Mount Rundle is an iconic mountain that extends from Canmore to Banff and is one of the first mountains visitors see when visiting the Bow Valley and Banff National Park. The series of eleven peaks was first traversed in the 1960s over several days, since whittled to under twenty-four hours.

On a whim, during the summer of 2015, Ryan Atkins and I crossed it from east to west in record-setting time, to the surprise of both of us. The route is exposed in places, and I strongly recommend the use of climbing gear, or at the very least a light rappeling rope. We are now working on setting the winter record and are currently zero out of one. It is also the subject of my documentary film *40 Winters*.

BIGGEST MINDFUCK

World's Toughest Mudder—Henderson, Nevada

Nobody likes mind games, but this twenty-four-hour obstacle course race requires you to do as many laps as possible of an 8 km loop during this time. You're challenged physically by the obstacles and the weather (once the sun goes down, it's anyone's guess as to what the temperature will be), as well as mentally and emotionally by having to repeat the obstacles—including ones you will grow to hate, or begin to fail as you weaken. Doing laps has always been hard for me, as each pass through is a chance to sit and take a break—or simply give up. Twice I've run in the top five for the first twelve hours, only to blow up on the back half and either give in or slow to a crawl. This is one I vow to get right before I die!

ACKNOWLEDGMENTS

Growing up, I used to hear the term "self-made man" thrown around frequently and held as a standard to strive for. There was something special about becoming successful through your own hard work rather than relying on others to provide advantages. I've realized that despite the pervasiveness of this ideology, it's a myth. Nobody makes it on their own. Not in business, sport, academia, spirituality, or love. I've been fortunate to receive an overabundance of help along my journey thus far, and many individuals have been instrumental in shaping me and my life's path. My family has provided immeasurable support for all of my pursuits since day one. While I might have taken it for granted in my younger years, I now reflect fondly, and with gratitude, on the support and sacrifice shown by my parents. For all of the athletic accolades that I've received through the years I can only smile, as my sisters are the truly gifted athletes in the family—I only got here because I kept going when my competition quit.

Writing this book was quite the learning experience, and I wouldn't have been successful without the help and guidance of Brad Wilson at HarperCollins. Although I'd written numerous articles and academic papers, this experience would have been a nonstarter without his guidance. Michael Vlessides contributed to the early structure and helped set me on the right track to begin writing, while Erin Parker was instrumental in editing the manuscript and in guiding me back to the themes of the book when I strayed. I also extend my thanks to the many additional members of the HarperCollins team who assisted in bringing this book to life.

This book exists in large part due to the series *Boundless*, and *Boundless* would not have been possible without the help of my friends and cocreators Josh and Jordan Eady. This three-year journey was enriched by the participation of my longtime friend Paul (Turbo) Trebilcock, Rory Bosio, Hunter McIntyre, Steven Bray, Merewyn Benyon, Brian Stewart, Wes Legge, and Josh Rainhard. I'd like to thank the staff at HLP+Partners—in particular Lee, Henry, Angela, and Nate—for all of their help and support along the way.

Adventure Science is my true passion and an extension of who I am as a person. I've been extremely fortunate to have developed lifelong friendships through these fascinating projects, and I would like to thank everyone who has participated since 2008. Although the list is long, there are several people who warrant a special mention, including Keith Szlater, Jim Mandelli, Richard Rothaus, Tim Puetz, Melissa Stewart, Ian MacNairn, Helene Dumais, Luis Moreira, Tyler LeBlanc, Liz Barney, Travis Steffans, Mark Tarnopolsky, and Chris Killian.

My journey as an entrepreneur, and my experience with Stoked Oats, has been made richer thanks to my two business partners, Brad Slessor and Shaun Stevens. I'd like to thank them both for their support while I vanished for weeks at a time to film *Boundless*, lead an Adventure Science project, or move to a rural farm in western Quebec. Their support and tolerance of my lifestyle has not gone unnoticed. We started as friends back in 2011 and we continue as friends. I hope this never changes. In 2015 we took on a small group of investors to help grow the business, and I have been grateful for their support and wisdom since then. I would also like to thank Clay Gillies at Planet Foods for taking a chance on us back in 2012 and helping to guide the development of Stoked Oats' brand.

The life I lead has certainly followed a very tortuous path, but it has allowed me to meet many people who have become friends and mentors, and who have profoundly inspired, enabled, and empowered me in many ways—be it through sport, business, academia, or simply being a good friend. Thank you to my friends, colleagues, coaches, academic supervisors and mentors, sponsors, training partners, and extended family for the support you have shown me and for teaching me, and constantly reminding me, how to live an incredible life.

The gear requirements for *Boundless* and Adventure Science are both extensive and expensive, but thankfully, many great companies stepped in to help through sponsorships. Merrell has outfitted me for many years and I am extremely grateful for the privilege of representing such a great brand. Farm to Feet makes the best socks on the market and has generously supported my racing and Adventure Science projects. I am also grateful to Suunto, Jimmy Lewis boards, Giro, CamelBak, Smith Optics, Salomon, Canada Satellite, Opus Bikes, Honey Stinger, and GoMacro for their support.

Finally, although I am not one to discuss matters of the heart—thank you, Chanelle. Your passion and drive to make the world a better place with a brighter future is both inspiring and motivational. You have also helped me to grow emotionally, and while difficult at times—what a wonderful gift you have given me. I look forward to a lifetime of love, adventure, and growth with you.